STAND OUT

Evidence-Based Learning for College and Career Readiness

1

THIRD EDITION

ROB JENKINS

STACI JOHNSON

NATIONAL
GEOGRAPHIC
LEARNING

CENGAGE
Learning·

Australia • Brazil • Mexico • Singapore • United Kingdom • United States

**Stand Out 1: Evidence-Based Learning
for College and Career Readiness,
Third Edition**
Rob Jenkins and Staci Johnson

Publisher: Sherrise Roehr

Executive Editor: Sarah Kenney

Senior Development Editor: Margarita Matte

Development Editor: Lewis Thompson

Director of Global Marketing: Ian Martin

Executive Marketing Manager: Ben Rivera

Product Marketing Manager: Dalia Bravo

Director of Content and Media Production:
    Michael Burggren

Production Manager: Daisy Sosa

Media Researcher: Leila Hishmeh

Senior Print Buyer: Mary Beth Hennebury

Cover and Interior Designer:
    Brenda Carmichael

Composition: Lumina

Cover Image: Portra Images/Getty Images

Bottom Images: (Left to Right) Jay B Sauceda/
    Getty Images; Tripod/Getty Images;
    Portra Images/Getty Images; James Porter/
    Getty Images; Mark Edward Atkinson/
    Tracey Lee/Getty Images; Hero Images/
    Getty Images; Jade/Getty Images; Seth Joel/
    Getty Images; LWA/Larry Williams/
    Getty Images; Dimitri Otis/Getty Images

For product information and technology assistance, contact us at
Cengage Learning Customer & Sales Support, 1-800-354-9706

For permission to use material from this text or product, submit all requests
online at **cengage.com/permissions**

Further permissions questions can be emailed to
permissionrequest@cengage.com

Student Book
ISBN 13: 978-1-337-90099-7

National Geographic Learning/Cengage Learning
20 Channel Center Street
Boston, MA 02210
USA

Cengage Learning is a leading provider of customized learning solutions with
office locations around the globe, including Singapore, the United Kingdom,
Australia, Mexico, Brazil, and Japan.

Cengage Learning products are represented in Canada by Nelson Education, Ltd.

Visit National Geographic Learning online at **ngl.Cengage.com**
Visit our corporate website at **www.cengage.com**

Printed in China
Print Number: 03   Print Year: 2019

ACKNOWLEDGMENTS

Ellen Albano
Mcfatter Technical College, Davie, FL

Esther Anaya-Garcia
Glendale Community College, Glendale, AZ

Carol Bellamy
Prince George's Community College, Largo, MD

Gail Bier
Atlantic Technical College, Coconut Creek, FL

Kathryn Black
Myrtle Beach Family Learning Center, Myrtle Beach, SC

Claudia Brantley
College of Southern Nevada, Las Vegas, NV

Dr. Joan-Yvette Campbell
Lindsey Hopkins Technical College, Miami, FL

Maria Carmen Iglesias
Miami Senior Adult Educational Center, Miami, FL

Lee Chen
Palomar College, San Marcos, CA

Casey Cahill
Atlantic Technical College, Coconut Creek, FL

Maria Dillehay
Burien Job Training and Education Center, Goodwill, Seattle, WA

Irene Fjaerestad
Olympic College, Bremerton, WA

Eleanor Forfang-Brockman
Tarrant County College, Fort Worth, Texas

Jesse Galdamez
San Bernardino Adult School, San Bernardino, CA

Anna Garoz
Lindsey Hopkins Technical Education Center, Miami, FL

Maria Gutierrez
Miami Sunset Adult, Miami, FL

Noel Hernandez
Palm Beach County Public Schools, Palm Beach County, FL

Kathleen Hiscock
Portland Adult Education, Portland, ME

Frantz Jean-Louis
The English Center, Miami, FL

Annette Johnson
Sheridan Technical College, Hollywood, FL

Ginger Karaway
Gateway Technical College, Kenosha, WI

Judy Martin-Hall
Indian River State College, Fort Pierce, FL

Toni Molinaro
Dixie Hollins Adult Education Center, St Petersburg, FL

Tracey Person
Cape Cod Community College, Hyannis, MA

Celina Paula
Miami-Dade County Public Schools, Miami, FL

Veronica Pavon-Baker
Miami Beach Adult, Miami, FL

Ileana Perez
Robert Morgan Technical College, Miami, FL

Neeta Rancourt
Atlantic Technical College, Coconut Creek, FL

Brenda Roland
Joliet Junior College, Joliet, IL

Hidelisa Sampson
Las Vegas Urban League, Las Vegas, NV

Lisa Schick
James Madison University, Harrisonburg, VA

Rob Sheppard
Quincy Asian Resources, Quincy, MA

Sydney Silver
Burien Job Training and Education Center, Goodwill, Seattle, WA

Teresa Tamarit
Miami Senior Adult Educational Center, Miami, FL

Cristina Urena
Atlantic Technical College, Fort Lauderdale, FL

Pamela Jo Wilson
Palm Beach County Public Schools, Palm Beach County, FL

ABOUT THE AUTHORS

Rob Jenkins

I love teaching. I love to see the expressions on my students' faces when the light goes on and their eyes show such sincere joy of learning. I knew the first time I stepped into an ESL classroom that this is where I needed to be and I have never questioned that resolution. I have worked in business, sales, and publishing, and I've found challenge in all, but nothing can compare to the satisfaction of reaching people in such a personal way.

Staci Johnson

Ever since I can remember, I've been fascinated with other cultures and languages. I love to travel and every place I go, the first thing I want to do is meet the people, learn their language, and understand their culture. Becoming an ESL teacher was a perfect way to turn what I love to do into my profession. There's nothing more incredible than the exchange of teaching and learning from one another that goes on in an ESL classroom. And there's nothing more rewarding than helping a student succeed.

Along with the inclusion of National Geographic content, the third edition of **Stand Out** boasts of several innovations. In response to initiatives regarding the development of more complexity with reading and encouraging students to interact more with reading texts, we are proud to introduce new rich reading sections that allow students to discuss topics relevant to a global society. We have also introduced new National Geographic videos that complement the life-skill videos **Stand Out** introduced in the second edition and which are now integrated into the student books. We don't stop there; **Stand Out** has even more activities that require critical and creative thinking that serve to maximize learning and prepare students for the future. The third edition also has online workbooks. **Stand Out** was the first mainstream ESL textbook for adults to introduce a lesson plan format, hundreds of customizable worksheets, and project-based instruction. The third edition expands on these features in its mission to provide rich learning opportunities that can be exploited in different ways. We believe that with the innovative approach that made **Stand Out** a leader from its inception, the many new features, and the new look; programs, teachers, and students will find great success!

Stand Out Mission Statement:

Our goal is to give students challenging opportunities to be successful in their language learning experience so they develop confidence and become independent lifelong learners.

TO THE TEACHER

ABOUT THE SERIES

The **Stand Out** series is designed to facilitate *active* learning within life-skill settings that lead students to career and academic pathways. Each student book and its supplemental components in the six-level series expose students to competency areas most useful and essential for newcomers with careful treatment of level appropriate but challenging materials. Students grow academically by developing essential literacy and critical thinking skills that will help them find personal success in a changing and dynamic world.

THE STAND OUT PHILOSOPHY

Integrated Skills

In each of the five lessons of every unit, skills are introduced as they might be in real language use. They are in context and not separated into different sections of the unit. We believe that for real communication to occur, the classroom should mirror real-life as much as possible.

Objective Driven Activities

Every lesson in **Stand Out** is driven by a performance objective. These objectives have been carefully selected to ensure they are measurable, accessible to students at their particular level, and relevant to students and their lives. Good objectives lead to effective learning. Effective objectives also lead to appropriate self, student, and program assessment which is increasingly required by state and federal mandates.

Lesson Plan Sequencing

Stand Out follows an established sequence of activities that provides students with the tools they need to have in order to practice and apply the skills required in the objective. A pioneer in Adult Education for introducing the Madeline Hunter WIPPEA lesson plan model into textbooks, **Stand Out** continues to provide a clear and easy-to-follow system for presenting and developing English language skills. The WIPPEA model follows six steps:

- **W**arm up and Review
- **I**ntroduction
- **P**resentation
- **P**ractice
- **E**valuation
- **A**pplication

Learning And Acquisition

In **Stand Out**, the recycling of skills is emphasized. Students must learn and practice the same skills multiple times in various contexts to actually acquire them. Practicing a skill one time is rarely sufficient for acquisition and rarely addresses diverse student needs and learning styles.

Critical Thinking

Critical thinking has been defined in various ways and sometimes so broadly that any activity could be classified to meet the criteria. To be clear and to draw attention to the strong critical thinking activities in **Stand Out,** we define these activities as *tasks that require learners to think deeper than the superficial vocabulary and meaning.* Activities such as ranking, making predictions, analyzing, or solving problems, demand that students think beyond the surface. Critical thinking is highlighted throughout so the instructor can be confident that effective learning is going on.

Learner-Centered, Cooperative, and Communicative Activities

Stand Out provides ample opportunities for students to develop interpersonal skills and to practice new vocabulary through graphic organizers and charts like VENN diagrams, graphs, classifying charts, and mind maps. The lesson planners provide learner-centered approaches in every lesson. Students are asked to rank items, make decisions, and negotiate amongst other things.

Dialogues are used to prepare students for these activities in the low levels and fewer dialogues are used at the higher levels where students have already acquired the vocabulary and rudimentary conversation skills.

Activities should provide opportunities for students to speak in near authentic settings so they have confidence to perform outside the classroom. This does not mean that dialogues and other mechanical activities are not used to prepare students for cooperative activities, but these mechanical activities do not foster conversation. They merely provide the first tools students need to go beyond mimicry.

Assessment

Instructors and students should have a clear understanding of what is being taught and what is expected. In **Stand Out**, objectives are clearly stated so that target skills can be effectively assessed throughout.

Formative assessments are essential. Pre and post-assessments can be given for units or sections of the book through *ExamView*—a program that makes developing tests easy and effective. These tests can be created to appear like standardized tests, which are important for funding and to help students prepare.

Finally, *learner logs* allow students to self-assess, document progress, and identify areas that might require additional attention.

SUPPLEMENTAL COMPONENTS

The **Stand Out** series is a comprehensive one-stop for all student needs. There is no need to look any further than the resources offered.

Stand Out Lesson Planners

The lesson planners go beyond merely describing activities in the student book by providing teacher support, ideas, and guidance for the entire class period.

- **Standards correlations** for **CCRS, CASAS,** and **SCANS** are identified for each lesson.
- **Pacing Guides** help with planning by giving instructors suggested durations for each activity and a selection of activities for different class lengths.
- **Teacher Tips** provide point-of-use pedagogical comments and best practices.
- **At-A-Glance Lesson Openers** provide the instructor with everything that will be taught in a particular lesson. Elements include: the agenda, the goal, grammar, pronunciation, academic strategies, critical thinking elements, correlations to standards, and resources.
- **Suggested Activities** go beyond what is shown in the text providing teachers with ideas that will stimulate them to come up with their own.
- **Listening Scripts** are integrated into the unit pages for easy access.

Stand Out Workbook

The workbook in the third edition takes the popular **Stand Out Grammar Challenge** and expands it to include vocabulary building, life-skill development, and grammar practice associated directly with each lesson in the student book.

Stand Out Online Workbook

One of the most important innovations new to the third edition of **Stand Out** is the online workbook. This workbook provides unique activities that are closely related to the student book and gives students opportunities to have access to audio and video.

The online workbook provides opportunities for students to practice and improve digital literacy skills essential for 21st century learners. These skills are essential for standardized computer and online testing. Scores in these tests will improve when students can concentrate on the content and not so much on the technology.

Activity Bank

The Activity Bank is an online feature that provides several hundred multilevel worksheets per level to enhance the already rich materials available through **Stand Out**.

DVD Program

The **Stand Out Lifeskills Video Program** continues to be available with eight episodes per level; however, now the worksheets are part of the student books with additional help in the lesson planners.

New to the third edition of **Stand Out** are two National Geographic videos per level. Each video is accompanied by four pages of instruction and activities with support in the lesson planners.

Examview

ExamView is a program that provides customizable test banks and allows instructors to make lesson, unit, and program tests quickly.

STANDARDS AND CORRELATIONS

Stand Out is the pioneer in establishing a foundation of standards within each unit and through every objective. The standards movement in the United States is as dominant today as it was when **Stand Out** was first published. Schools and programs must be aware of on-going local and federal initiatives and make attempts to meet ever-changing requirements.

In the first edition of **Stand Out**, we identified direct correlations to SCANS, EFF, and CASAS standards. *The Secretaries Commission on Achieving Necessary Skills* or SCANS and *Equipped for the Future* or EFF standards are still important and are identified in every lesson of **Stand Out**. These skills include the basic skills, interpersonal skills, and problem-solving skills necessary to be successful in the workplace, in school, and in the community. **Stand Out** was also developed with a thorough understanding of objectives established by the *Comprehensive Adult Student Assessment Systems* or CASAS. Many programs have experienced great success with their CASAS scores using **Stand Out**, and these objectives continue to be reflected in the third edition.

Today, a new emphasis on critical thinking and complexity has swept the nation. Students are expected to think for themselves more now than ever before. They must also interact with reading texts at a higher level. These new standards and expectations are highly visible in the third edition and include *College and Career Readiness Standards.*

Stand Out offers a complete set of correlations online for all standards to demonstrate how closely we align with state and federal guidelines.

IMPORTANT INNOVATIONS TO THE THIRD EDITION

New Look
Although the third edition of **Stand Out** boasts of the same lesson plan format and task-based activities that made it one of the most popular books in adult education, it now has an updated look with the addition of the National Geographic content which will capture the attention of the instructor and every student.

Critical Thinking
With the advent of new federal and state initiatives, teachers need to be confident that students will use critical thinking skills when learning. This has always been a goal in **Stand Out**, but now those opportunities are highlighted in each lesson.

College And Career Readiness Skills
These skills are also identified by critical thinking strategies and academic-related activities, which are found throughout **Stand Out**. New to the third edition is a special reading section in each unit that challenges students and encourages them to develop reading strategies within a rich National Geographic environment.

Stand Out Workbook
The print workbook is now more extensive and complete with vocabulary, life skills, and grammar activities to round out any program. Many instructors might find these pages ideal for homework, but they of course can be used for additional practice within the classroom.

Media And Online Support
Media and online support includes audio, video, online workbooks, presentation tools, and multi-level worksheets, ExamView, and standards correlations.

CONTENTS

Numeracy/ Academic Skills	CCRS	SCANS	CASAS
• Clarification strategies • Pronunciation • Focused listening	RI1, SL2, SL3, L2, RF2	• Listening • Speaking • Sociability	**1:** 0.1.1, 0.1.4, 0.2.1 **2:** 0.1.2, 0.1.4, 0.2.2 **3:** 0.1.5, 0.1.6, 2.2.1
• Focused listening • Predicting • Reviewing • Self-evaluation	RI1, R12, RI3, RI5, RI7, W2, SL1, SL2, SL4, L1, L2, L5, RF2, RF3	**Most SCANS are incorporated into this unit, with an emphasis on:** • Acquiring information • Interpreting and evaluating information • Writing (Technology is optional.)	**1:** 0.1.2, 0.2.1, 0.1.4, 0.2.1 **2:** 0.1.2, 0.1.3, 1.1.4 **3:** 0.1.2 **4:** 0.2.4 **5:** 2.3.1 **R:** 0.1.2, 0.1.3, 0.2.1, 0.2.4, 1.1.4, 2.3.1, 4.8.1 **TP:** 0.1.2, 0.1.3, 0.2.1, 0.2.4, 1.1.4, 2.3.1
• Categorizing • Classifying • Focused listening • Graphs • Predicting • Reviewing • Self-evaluation	RI1, RI2, RI3, RI5, RI7, SL1, SL2, SL4, L1, L2, L5, RF2, RF3	**Most SCANS are incorporated into this unit, with an emphasis on:** • Allocating money • Serving customers • Organizing and maintaining information • Decision making (Technology is optional.)	**1:** 1.1.3, 1.3.7, 2.5.4 **2:** 1.3.3, 1.3.8, 1.3.9, 1.6.4 **3:** 1.2.1, 1.3.9 **4:** 1.3.9 **5:** 0.1.2, 1.1.9, 1.3.9 **R:** 0.1.2, 1.1.9, 1.2.1, 1.3.3, 1.3.8, 1.3.9, 1.6.4 **TP:** 0.1.2, 1.1.9, 1.2.1, 1.3.3, 1.3.8, 1.3.9, 1.6.4, 4.8.1

CONTENTS

Numeracy/ Academic Skills	CCRS	SCANS	CASAS
• Brainstorming • Classifying • Critical thinking • Focused listening • Making graphs • Predicting • Reviewing • Self-evaluation	RI1, RI2, RI5, RI7, RI9, SL1, SL2, SL4, L1, L2, L4, L5, RF2, RF3	**Most SCANS are incorporated into this unit, with an emphasis on:** • Allocating money • Understanding systems • Creative thinking • Seeing things in the mind's eye (Technology is optional.)	**1:** 1.3.8, 7.2.3 **2:** 1.2.1, 1.2.4, 1.3.8 **3:** 0.1.2, 1.1.7, 1.3.8, 7.2.6 **4:** 1.1.3, 1.2.1, 1.2.2, 1.3.8 **5:** 1.3.8, 2.6.4, 7.2.3 **R:** 0.1.2, 1.1.3, 1.1.7, 1.2.1, 1.2.2, 1.2.4, 2.6.4 **TP:** 0.1.2, 1.1.3, 1.1.7, 1.2.1, 1.2.2, 1.2.4, 2.6.4, 4.8.1
• Classifying • Focused listening • Pie charts • Reviewing • Self-evaluation • Venn diagrams	RI1, RI2, RI5, RI7, W2, SL1, SL2, SL4, L1, L2, L4, L5, RF2, RF3	**Most SCANS are incorporated into this unit, with an emphasis on:** • Acquiring and evaluating information • Creative thinking • Seeing things in the mind's eye (Technology is optional.)	**1:** 1.1.3, 1.4.1 **2:** 1.1.3, 1.4.1, 4.8.1, 7.2.3 **3:** 1.4.2 **4:** 1.4.2 **5:** 1.4.1, 1.4.2, 2.2.1 **R:** 1.4.1, 1.4.2 **TP:** 1.4.1, 1.4.2, 4.8.1
• Brainstorming • Classifying • Focused listening • Reviewing • Scanning for information • Self-evaluation	RI1, RI2, RI5, RI7, W2, SL1, SL2, SL4, L1, L2, L4, L5, RF3	**Most SCANS are incorporated into this unit, with an emphasis on:** • Acquiring and evaluating information • Reading • Seeing things in the mind's eye • Sociability (Technology is optional.)	**1:** 1.1.3, 2.5.1, 2.5.3, 7.4.4 **2:** 1.1.3, 1.9.1, 1.9.4, 2.2.1, 2.2.2, 2.2.5 **3:** 1.3.7, 2.2.1, 2.5.4 **4:** 2.1.7, 2.1.8 **5:** 0.2.3 **R:** 0.2.3, 1.1.3, 2.1.7, 2.1.8, 1.9.1, 2.2.2 **TP:** 0.2.3, 1.1.3, 2.1.7, 2.1.8, 1.9.1, 2.2.2, 4.8.1

CONTENTS

Numeracy/ Academic Skills	CCRS	SCANS	CASAS
• Clarification strategies • Focused listening • Graphs • Predicting • Ranking • Reviewing • Self-evaluation • VENN diagrams	RI1, RI2, RI5, RI7, SL1, SL2, SL4, L1, L2, L4, L5, RF2, RF3	**Most SCANS are incorporated into this unit, with an emphasis on:** • Interpreting and communicating information • Understanding systems • Decision making (Technology is optional.)	**1:** 3.1.1 **2:** 3.1.1, 6.6.5 **3:** 0.1.3, 3.3.1, 3.3.2, 3.3.3 **4:** 0.1.2, 2.5.1 **5:** 1.1.3, 3.5.9, 7.1.1 **R:** 2.5.1, 3.1.1, 3.3.1, 3.3.2, 3.3.3, 3.5.9 **TP:** 2.5.1, 3.1.1, 3.3.1, 3.3.2, 3.3.3, 3.5.9, 4.8.1
• Clarification strategies • Classifying • Focused listening • Peer editing • Ranking • Reviewing • Scanning • Self-evaluation • VENN diagrams	RI1, RI2, RI5, RI7, RI9, W2, SL1, SL2, SL3, SL4, L1, L2, L5, RF2, RF3	**Most SCANS are incorporated into this unit, with an emphasis on:** • Organizing and maintaining information • Understanding systems • Creative thinking • Decision making (Technology is optional.)	**1:** 4.1.8 **2:** 4.1.3, 4.1.6, 4.1.8 **3:** 4.1.2, 4.1.8 **4:** 0.1.1, 0.1.6, 4.1.5, 4.6.1 **5:** 4.4.1, 4.4.4 **R:** 4.1.2, 4.1.3, 4.1.6, 4.1.8, 4.1.5, 4.4.1, 4.4.4, 4.6.1 **TP:** 4.1.2, 4.1.3, 4.1.6, 4.1.8, 4.1.5, 4.4.1, 4.4.4, 4.6.1, 4.8.1
• Focused listening • Note-taking • Organizational strategies • Predicting • Reviewing • Self-evaluation	RI1, RI2, RI5, RI7, W2, SL1, SL2, L1, L2, L4, L5, RF3	**Most SCANS are incorporated into this unit, with an emphasis on:** • Understanding systems • Monitoring and correcting performance • Knowing how to learn • Self-management (Technology is optional.)	**1:** 7.4.1 **2:** 7.1.4, 7.4.1, 7.4.9 **3:** 2.5.5, 7.1.1 **4:** 7.1.1, 7.5.1 **5:** 7.1.1, 7.1.2 **R:** 7.1.1, 7.1.4, 7.4.1, 7.4.9, 7.5.1 **TP:** 4.8.1, 7.1.1, 7.1.4, 7.4.1, 7.4.9, 7.5.1

Appendices

For other national and state specific standards, please visit: **www.NGL.Cengage.com/SO3**

INTRODUCING
STAND OUT, Third Edition!

Stand Out is a six-level, standards-based ESL series for adult education with a proven track record of successful results. The new edition of *Stand Out* continues to provide students with the foundations and tools needed to achieve success in life, college, and career.

Stand Out now integrates real-world content from National Geographic

UNIT **1**
Balancing Your Life

UNIT OUTCOMES
- Analyze and create schedules
- Identify goals and obstacles and suggest solutions
- Write about a personal goal
- Analyze study habits
- Manage time

Look at the photo and answer the questions.
1. What do you think the people are doing?
2. What activities do you do every day?
3. What do you want to do in the future?

Construction workers on beams at the top of the Stratosphere Tower in Las Vegas.

- *Stand Out* now integrates high-interest, real-world content from National Geographic which enhances its proven approach to lesson planning and instruction. A stunning National Geographic image at the beginning of each unit introduces the theme and engages learners in meaningful conversations right from the start.

Stand Out supports college and career readiness

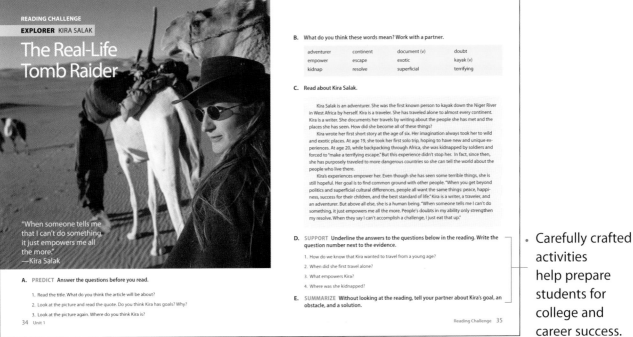

READING CHALLENGE
EXPLORER KIRA SALAK

The Real-Life Tomb Raider

"When someone tells me that I can't do something, it just empowers me all the more."
—Kira Salak

A. PREDICT Answer the questions before you read.

1. Read the title. What do you think the article will be about?
2. Look at the picture and read the quote. Do you think Kira has goals? Why?
3. Look at the picture again. Where do you think Kira is?

34 Unit 1

B. What do you think these words mean? Work with a partner.

adventurer	continent	document (v)	doubt
empower	escape	exotic	kayak (v)
kidnap	resolve	superficial	terrifying

C. Read about Kira Salak.

Kira Salak is an adventurer. She was the first known person to kayak down the Niger River in West Africa by herself. Kira is a traveler. She has traveled alone to almost every continent. Kira is a writer. She documents her travels by writing about the people she has met and the places she has seen. How did she become all of these things?

Kira wrote her first short story at the age of six. Her imagination always took her to wild and exotic places. At age 19, she took her first solo trip, hoping to have new and unique experiences. At age 20, while backpacking through Africa, she was kidnapped by soldiers and forced to "make a terrifying escape." But this experience didn't stop her. In fact, since then, she has purposely traveled to more dangerous countries so she can tell the world about the people who live there.

Kira's experiences empower her. Even though she has seen some terrible things, she is still hopeful. Her goal is to find common ground with other people. "When you get beyond politics and superficial cultural differences, people all want the same things: peace, happiness, success for their children, and the best standard of life." Kira is a writer, a traveler, and an adventurer. But above all else, she is a human being. "When someone tells me I can't do something, it just empowers me all the more. People's doubts in my ability only strengthen my resolve. When they say I can't accomplish a challenge, I just eat that up."

D. SUPPORT Underline the answers to the questions below in the reading. Write the question number next to the evidence.

1. How do we know that Kira wanted to travel from a young age?
2. When did she first travel alone?
3. What empowers Kira?
4. Where was she kidnapped?

E. SUMMARIZE Without looking at the reading, tell your partner about Kira's goal, an obstacle, and a solution.

Reading Challenge 35

- Carefully crafted activities help prepare students for college and career success.

- **NEW Reading Challenge** in every unit features a fascinating story about a **National Geographic explorer** to immerse learners in authentic content.

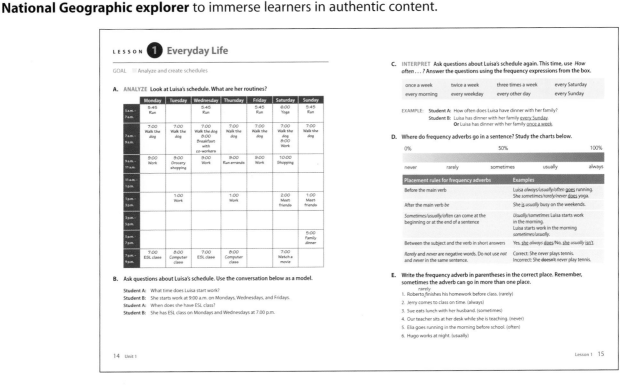

LESSON **1** Everyday Life

GOAL ▪ Analyze and create schedules

A. ANALYZE Look at Luisa's schedule. What are her routines?

	Monday	Tuesday	Wednesday	Thursday	Friday	Saturday	Sunday
5 a.m.–7 a.m.	5:45 Run		5:45 Run		5:45 Run	8:00 Yoga	5:45 Run
7 a.m.–9 a.m.	7:00 Walk the dog	7:00 Walk the dog	7:00 Walk the dog 8:00 Breakfast with co-workers	7:00 Walk the dog	7:00 Walk the dog	7:00 Walk the dog 8:00 Work	7:00 Walk the dog
9 a.m.–11 a.m.	9:00 Work	9:00 Grocery shopping	9:00 Work	9:00 Run errands	9:00 Work	10:00 Shopping	
11 a.m.–1 p.m.							
1 p.m.–3 p.m.		1:00 Work		1:00 Work		2:00 Meet friends	1:00 Meet friends
3 p.m.–5 p.m.							
5 p.m.–7 p.m.							5:00 Family dinner
7 p.m.–9 p.m.	7:00 ESL class	8:00 Computer class	7:00 ESL class	8:00 Computer class	7:00 Watch a movie		

B. Ask questions about Luisa's schedule. Use the conversation below as a model.

Student A: What time does Luisa start work?
Student B: She starts work at 9:00 a.m. on Mondays, Wednesdays, and Fridays.
Student A: When does she have ESL class?
Student B: She has ESL class on Mondays and Wednesdays at 7:00 p.m.

14 Unit 1

C. INTERPRET Ask questions about Luisa's schedule again. This time, use *How often . . . ?* Answer the questions using the frequency expressions from the box.

| once a week | twice a week | three times a week | every Saturday |
| every morning | every weekday | every other day | every Sunday |

EXAMPLE: Student A: How often does Luisa have dinner with her family?
Student B: Luisa has dinner with her family *every Sunday.*
Or Luisa has dinner with her family *once a week.*

D. Where do frequency adverbs go in a sentence? Study the charts below.

0%		50%		100%
never	rarely	sometimes	usually	always

Placement rules for frequency adverbs	Examples
Before the main verb	Luisa *always/usually/often* goes running. She *sometimes/rarely/never* does yoga.
After the main verb *be*	She *is usually* busy on the weekends.
Sometimes/usually/often can come at the beginning or at the end of a sentence.	*Usually/sometimes* Luisa starts work in the morning. Luisa starts work in the morning *sometimes/usually.*
Between the subject and the verb in short answers	Yes, she *always* does/No, she *usually* isn't.
Rarely and *never* are negative words. Do not use *not* and *never* in the same sentence.	Correct: She *never* plays tennis. Incorrect: She doesn't *never* play tennis.

E. Write the frequency adverb in parentheses in the correct place. Remember, sometimes the adverb can go in more than one place.

1. Roberto finishes his homework before class. (rarely)
2. Jerry comes to class on time. (always)
3. Sue eats lunch with her husband. (sometimes)
4. Our teacher sits at her desk while she is teaching. (never)
5. Elia goes running in the morning before school. (often)
6. Hugo works at night. (usually)

Lesson 1 15

- **EXPANDED Critical Thinking Activities** challenge learners to evaluate, analyze, and synthesize information to prepare them for the workplace and academic life.

- **NEW Video Challenge** showcases **National Geographic footage and explorers**, providing learners with the opportunity to synthesize what they have learned in prior units through the use of authentic content.

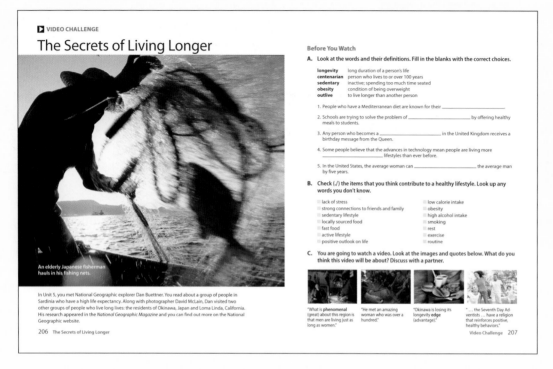

▶ VIDEO CHALLENGE

The Secrets of Living Longer

An elderly Japanese fisherman hauls in his fishing nets.

In Unit 5, you met National Geographic explorer Dan Buettner. You read about a group of people in Sardinia who have a high life expectancy. Along with photographer David McLain, Dan visited two other groups of people who live long lives: the residents of Okinawa, Japan and Loma Linda, California. His research appeared in the *National Geographic Magazine* and you can find out more on the National Geographic website.

206   The Secrets of Living Longer

Before You Watch

A. Look at the words and their definitions. Fill in the blanks with the correct choices.

longevity	long duration of a person's life
centenarian	person who lives to or over 100 years
sedentary	inactive; spending too much time seated
obesity	condition of being overweight
outlive	to live longer than another person

1. People who have a Mediterranean diet are known for their _____

2. Schools are trying to solve the problem of _____ by offering healthy meals to students.

3. Any person who becomes a _____ in the United Kingdom receives a birthday message from the Queen.

4. Some people believe that the advances in technology mean people are living more _____ lifestyles than ever before.

5. In the United States, the average woman can _____ the average man by five years.

B. Check (✓) the items that you think contribute to a healthy lifestyle. Look up any words you don't know.

- lack of stress
- strong connections to friends and family
- sedentary lifestyle
- locally sourced food
- fast food
- active lifestyle
- positive outlook on life
- low calorie intake
- obesity
- high alcohol intake
- smoking
- rest
- exercise
- routine

C. You are going to watch a video. Look at the images and quotes below. What do you think this video will be about? Discuss with a partner.

"What is **phenomenal** (great) about this region is that men are living just as long as women."

"He met an amazing woman who was over a hundred."

"Okinawa is losing its longevity **edge** (advantage)."

"... the Seventh Day Adventists ... have a religion that reinforces positive, healthy behaviors."

Video Challenge   207

LIFESKILLS ▶ My Schedule is Crazy

Before You Watch

A. Look at the picture and answer the questions.

1. What's wrong with Hector?

2. What do you think Naomi is saying to Hector?

While You Watch

B. ▶ Watch the video and complete the dialog.

Naomi: . . . you wouldn't skip a day of work, either. Treat your studies in the same way, and your grades will (1) _____improve_____

Hector: That's a great (2) _____, thanks.

Naomi: Well, now you know what you have to do. So go do it! If you get (3) _____ you'll feel more productive. Trust me!

Hector: (4) _____ give it a try. What have I got to lose, right?

Naomi: Good luck. Tell me how it's (5) _____ later on.

Hector: I (6) _____. Talk to you later.

Check Your Understanding

C. Circle the correct word to complete each sentence.

1. There's too much noise and it's difficult for Hector to (communicate/concentrate).

2. Hector says his (schedule/organization) is crazy and he has no time to study.

3. Naomi suggests that Hector (make time/write down) where and when he going to study.

4. A schedule will help Hector to (get organized/spend time with friends).

5. Naomi tells Hector a schedule will make him (productive/smarter).

Lifeskills Video   29

- The **Lifeskills Video** is a dramatic video series integrated into each unit of the student book that helps students learn natural spoken English and apply it to their everyday activities.

Pages shown are from *Stand Out*, Third Edition Level 3

- **NEW Online Workbook** engages students and supports the classroom by providing a wide variety of auto-graded interactive activities, an audio program, video from National Geographic, and pronunciation activities.

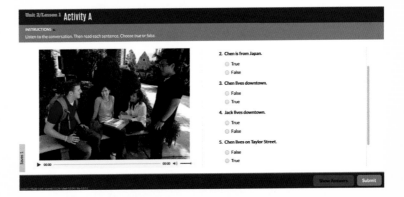

- **UPDATED Lesson Planner** includes correlations to **College and Career Readiness Standards (CCRS), CASAS, SCANS** and reference to **EL Civics** competencies to help instructors achieve the required standards.

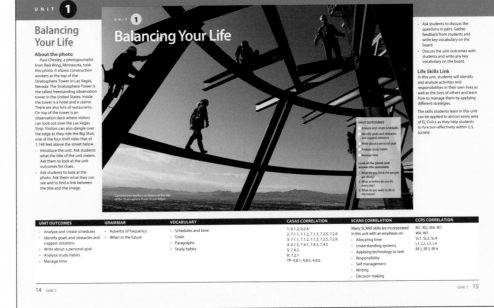

- **Teacher support** *Stand Out* continues to provide a wide variety of user-friendly tools and interactive activities that help teachers prepare students for success while keeping them engaged and motivated.

Stand Out supports teachers and learners

LEARNER COMPONENTS

- Student Book
- Online workbook powered by **My ELT**
- Print workbook

TEACHER COMPONENTS

- Lesson Planner
- Classroom DVD
- Assessment CD-ROM
- Teacher's companion site with Multi-Level Worksheets

Welcome

UNIT OUTCOMES

- Greet people
- Say and write phone numbers
- Follow instructions

LESSON **1** Hello!

GOAL ▪ Greet people

🎧 **A. Listen.**

CD 1
TR 1

B. Complete the conversations and practice them with a partner.

1. **Felipe:** _____. Welcome to our class.

   Student: Hello. Thank you.

2. **Gabriela:** Hi! _____How are you_____?

   Duong: Fine, thanks. _____?

3. **Eva:** _____. Welcome to our class.

   Student: Hi. Thank you.

C. Read the greetings.

hi	hello	welcome	How are you?
good morning	good afternoon	good evening	

D. Listen and complete the conversation.

Roberto: Hi. I'm Roberto. _____?

Gabriela: _____. My name is Gabriela. I'm fine, thanks.

Roberto: _____ to our class.

Gabriela: Thank you.

Roberto: Our teacher is Miss Smith.

E. Listen and repeat.

CD 1
TR 3

Hi! I'm Gabriela.
G-A-B-R-I-E-L-A.

Hello. I'm Duong.
D-U-O-N-G.

Can you repeat that?
Can you speak slower?
Can you spell that again?

F. Listen and repeat.

CD 1
TR 4

Aa	Bb	Cc	Dd	Ee	Ff
Gg	Hh	Ii	Jj	Kk	Ll
Mm	Nn	Oo	Pp	Qq	Rr
Ss	Tt	Uu	Vv	Ww	Xx
Yy	Zz				

CONTRACTIONS
/m/   I'm

G. Listen and write.

CD 1
TR 5

1. Hi! I'm _____.

2. Hello! My name is _____.

3. How are you? I'm _____.

4. Hi! My name is _____.

H. Greet five people in your class. Ask them to spell their names. Write their names.

1. _____

2. _____

3. _____

4. _____

5. _____

LESSON ② What's your number?

GOAL ▪ Say and write numbers

A. Look at the picture. Describe what you see. Say how many students there are. Say where the teacher is.

B. Read the paragraph. Circle the numbers.

> Welcome to Miss Smith's class. There are 12 students in the class. The students study for six hours every week. The school address is 19 Lincoln Street, Irvine, California 92602.

C. SURVEY Complete the chart about your class.

Teacher's name	
Number of students	
Number of hours	
Zip code	

D. Listen and practice saying the numbers 0 to 20.

0 zero/oh	1 one	2 two	3 three
4 four	5 five	6 six	7 seven
8 eight	9 nine	10 ten	11 eleven
12 twelve	13 thirteen	14 fourteen	15 fifteen
16 sixteen	17 seventeen	18 eighteen	19 nineteen
20 twenty			

E. Listen and write the numbers you hear. Then, spell them out.

1. _____5_____   _____five_____

2. _____   _____

3. _____   _____

4. _____   _____

5. _____   _____

6. _____   _____

F. Listen and write the missing numbers.

My name is Gabriela. My address is _____ Main Street. The zip

code is _____. My phone number is _____.

There are _____ students in my class.
          (Spell out)

G. **Read about Gabriela and Eva.**

Name: Gabriela Ramirez
Address: 14 Main Street
Zip code: 06119
Phone: 401-555-7248

Name: Eva Malinska
Address: 333 Western Circle
Zip code: 06119
Phone: 401-555-3534

H. **Look at the numbers. Write the information in the chart.**

2945 Broadway	916-555-2386	415-555-7869	72643
800-555-2675	9235 Sundry Way	98724	8 Palm Circle
213-555-5761	78231	9921 Johnson Street	23145

Address	Zip code	Phone
2945 Broadway		

I. **Write the numbers. Say the numbers to your partner. Listen and write your partner's numbers.**

	You	Your partner
1. The number of people in your family		
2. Your phone number		
3. Your address		
4. Your zip code		

GOAL ▦ Follow instructions

A. Write the words under the pictures.

listen	read	speak	write

1.

_____

2.

_____

3.

_____

4.

_____

🎧
CD 1
TR 9

B. Listen and point to the correct picture.

C. Complete the instructions. Use the words from the box in Exercise A.

1. _____ Write _____ your name on the paper.

2. _____ to the audio and repeat.

3. _____ your answers on the board.

4. _____ the story and answer the questions.

5. _____ with your partner about the picture.

D. **Match the sentences with the pictures. Write the letter.**

a.

b.

c.

d.

e.

f.

g.

h.

___d___ 1. Please stand up.

_____ 2. Please read.

_____ 3. Please sit down.

_____ 4. Please take out a sheet of paper.

_____ 5. Please open your book.

_____ 6. Please listen carefully.

_____ 7. Please write.

_____ 8. Please help Juana.

E. **Listen and follow the instructions.**

CD 1
TR 10

F. Read the conversation.

Teacher: Please open your
books to page
fifteen.

Student: What page?

Teacher: Page fifteen.
That's one, five.

Student: Thank you.

G. Practice with a partner.

**Student B's book is closed.
Student A says:**

1. Please open your book
to page six.

2. Please open your book to page fourteen.

3. Please open your book to Unit 4, Lesson 2.

4. Please open your book to the vocabulary list on pages 212 and 213.

H. Practice with a partner.

Student A's book is closed. Student B says:

1. Please open your book to page three.

2. Please open your book to page twelve.

3. Please open your book to Unit 7, Lesson 3.

4. Please open your book to the charts on page 214.

I. Give instructions to a partner.

1. Please stand up.

2. Please take out your book and open to page fifteen.

3. Please sit down.

4. Please write my name on a sheet of paper.

5. Please read my name.

J. Guess the instruction. Act out an instruction and your partner guesses it.

UNIT **1**

Talking with Others

Friends sit and talk as they fish at a lake in Alaska.

UNIT OUTCOMES

- Ask for and give personal information
- Describe people
- Describe family relationships
- Express preferences
- Plan a schedule

Look at the photo and answer the questions.

1. Where are they?
2. How old are they?
3. What do they look like?

LESSON 1 Where are you from?

GOAL ▪ Ask for and give personal information

A. **Look at the picture. Where is Roberto from?**

B. **INTERPRET** **Read more about Roberto.**

My name is <u>Roberto</u> <u>Garcia</u>. I'm a new student in this school. I'm from Mexico City, <u>Mexico</u>. I'm <u>43</u> years old and I'm <u>married</u>. I'm very happy in my new class.

C. **CLASSIFY** **Write the underlined words from Exercise B about Roberto in the chart below.**

First name	Last name	Country	Age	Marital status

D. **Complete the sentences about Roberto.**

(age)   1. Roberto Garcia is _____ years old.

(country)   2. He is from _____.

(marital status) 3. He is _____.

E. **Look at the pictures.**

single

divorced

married

F. **Match the questions with the answers.**

1. Where are you from?
2. What's your name?
3. Are you married?
4. How old are you?

a. Yes, I'm married.
b. I'm from Mexico.
c. I'm 43 years old.
d. Roberto.

CD 1
TR 11-13

G. **Listen and complete the missing information.**

1.

Name: _Eva Malinska_

Age: _____

Marital status: _____

Country: _____

2.

Name: _Gabriela Ramirez_

Age: _____

Marital status: _____

Country: _____

3.

Name: _Felipe Rodriguez_

Age: _____

Marital status: _____

Country: _____

H. Study the chart with your classmates and teacher.

Simple Present: *Be*			
Subject	*Be*	**Information**	**Example sentence**
I	am	43 years old	I **am** 43 years old.
He, She	is	single from Argentina	He **is** single. (Roberto **is** single.) She **is** from Argentina. (Gabriela **is** from Argentina.)
We, You, They	are	single married from Russia	We **are** single. You **are** married. They **are** from Russia.

I. Write sentences about the people below.

Trinh Hong
33 years old
Single
Cambodia

Duong Bui
33 years old
Married
Vietnam

Alan Hart
64 years old
Divorced
United States

1. (marital status) Duong _is married_ .
2. (marital status) Alan _is divorced_ .
3. (marital status) Trinh _is Single_ and Alan _is Divorced_ .
4. (age) Trinh and Duong _are 33 year old 33 years old_ .
5. (age) Alan _is 64 year old_ .
6. (country) Alan _is United state_ .

J. SURVEY In a group, interview three students. Complete the table.

What's your name?	Where are you from?	How old are you?	Are you married?

LESSON **2** What does he look like?

GOAL ▪ Describe people

A. INTERPRET Look at Felipe's license. Complete the sentences.

CALIFORNIA CLASS: C M1 *DMV*
DRIVER'S LICENSE

LIC. NUMBER: S7890123
FELIPE RODRIGUEZ
8220 State St.
San Francisco, CA 94160
Birth date: 6-23-90
Height: 5'11"   Weight: 175
Hair: Black   Eyes: Brown

Felipe Rodriguez

ISSUED: 09/07/15   EXPIRES: 06/23/20   NON-RESTRICTED

> **WRITE OUT**
> 5'11" = five feet, eleven inches
>   = five-eleven

1. Felipe is _five feet 11 inch_ tall.
2. He is _175_ pounds.
3. His hair is _Black_.
4. His eyes are _Brown_.
5. He is _29_ years old.
6. His address is _8220_ State Street.

> **HIS / HER**
> **Duong**
> **His** hair is black.
> **His** eyes are brown.
> **Eva**
> **Her** hair is white.
> **Her** eyes are blue.

B. Look at the licenses below. Complete the sentences about Duong and Eva.

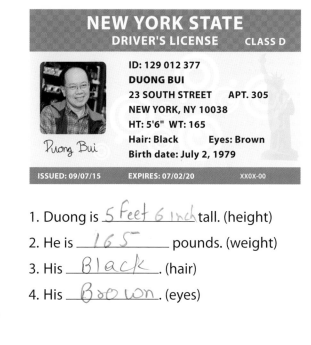

1. Duong is _5 feet 6 inch_ tall. (height)
2. He is _165_ pounds. (weight)
3. His _Black_. (hair)
4. His _Brown_. (eyes)

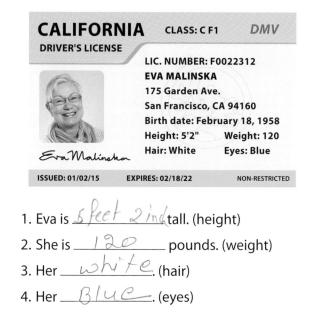

1. Eva is _5 feet 2 inch_ tall. (height)
2. She is _120_ pounds. (weight)
3. Her _white_. (hair)
4. Her _Blue_. (eyes)

C. Study the chart with your classmates and teacher.

Simple Present: *Have*		
Subject	**Verb**	**Example sentence**
I, You, We, They	have	I **have** black hair. You **have** white hair.
He, She, It	has	He **has** brown eyes. She **has** blue eyes.

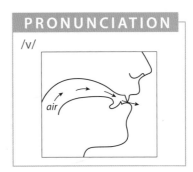

/v/

air

D. **CLASSIFY** Listen and complete the chart.

Name	Height	Hair	Eyes	Age
1. Roberto	5'11"	black	brown	43
2. Trinh				
3. Gabriela				
4. Alan				

E. Listen to and practice the conversation.

Student A: What does <u>Roberto</u> look like?

Student B: <u>He</u> has <u>black hair</u> and <u>brown eyes</u>.

Student A: How tall is <u>he</u>?

Student B: <u>He</u> is <u>five feet, eleven inches</u> tall.

Student A: Thank you.

F. Practice the conversation with information about Trinh, Gabriela, and Alan.

She has brown hair and brown eyes. She is tall.

G. Discuss the words with your classmates and teacher.

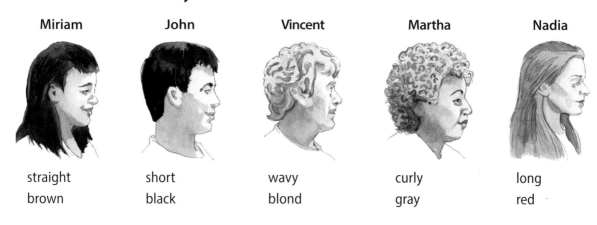

Miriam	John	Vincent	Martha	Nadia
straight	short	wavy	curly	long
brown	black	blond	gray	red

> **ADJECTIVES**
> Adjectives come before the noun. Always say colors just before the noun.
>   1   2
> Miriam has *straight brown* hair.

H. DESIGN In a group, choose and draw the best hair color and style for each face.

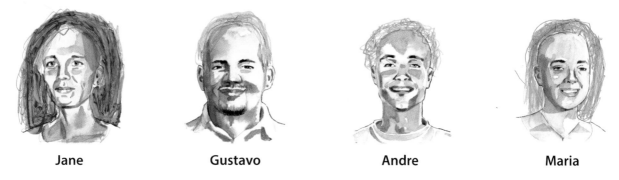

Jane	Gustavo	Andre	Maria

I. APPLY Complete the driver's license with your information.

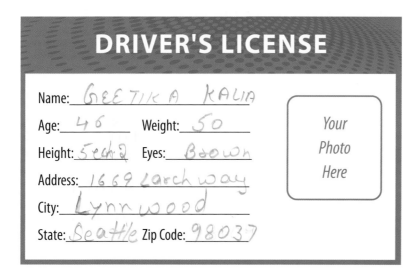

DRIVER'S LICENSE

Name: GEETIKA KALIA

Age: 46   Weight: 50

Height: 5 ech 2   Eyes: Brown

Address: 1669 Larch way

City: Lynnwood

State: Seattle   Zip Code: 98037

Your Photo Here

LESSON **3** Roberto's family

A. Look at the picture. Who is in the picture? What are they saying?

B. Listen to the conversation.

CD 1
TR 19

Roberto:	Duong, this is my mother, my father, and my sister.
Antonio:	Nice to meet you, Duong. Where are you from?
Duong:	I'm from Vietnam.
Antonio:	Do your parents live here in the United States?
Duong:	No. Right now they live in Vietnam.

C. Look at the people from the picture above. Write the words from the box under the pictures.

friend	son	parents	sister	brother

_____ _____

_____ _____

friend _____

D. Discuss the words with your classmates and teacher.

father	wife	children	grandson	uncle
mother	husband	grandfather	granddaughter	niece
brother	son	grandmother	aunt	nephew
sister	daughter			

E. **PREDICT** Look at the picture and write the names on the family tree. Then, listen to check your answers.

CD 1
TR 20

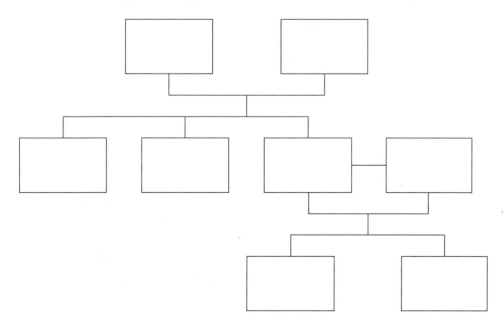

F. Practice the conversation.

Student A: Who is <u>Silvia</u>?
Student B: <u>Silvia is Roberto's wife</u>.

Student A: Who are <u>Antonio and Rebecca</u>?
Student B: They are <u>Roberto's parents</u>.

G. Work with a partner. Ask questions about Roberto's family on page 21.

H. CREATE Complete the family tree for your family.

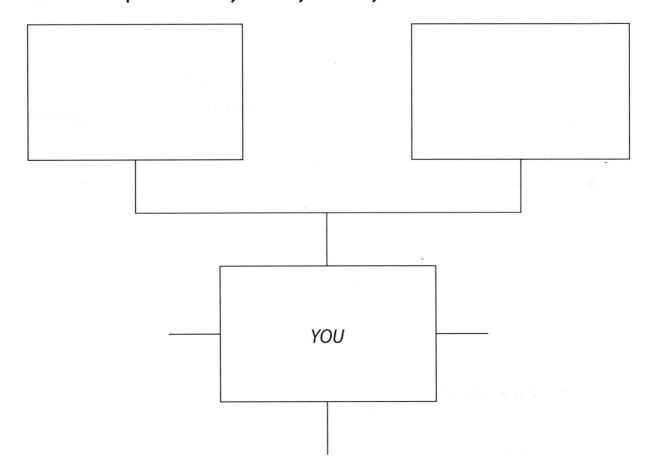

I. Find or draw a picture of your family and share it with the class.

GOAL ▪ Express preferences

🎧 **A.** **Listen. Put an *R* by things Roberto likes and an *S* by things Silvia likes. Roberto and Silvia both like some of them.**

movies ___R___   music ___S___   sports ___Both___

games ___R___   computers ___Both___   TV ___Both___

books ___R___   restaurants ___S___   parks ___S___

B. **Complete the sentences.**

1. Roberto likes ___movies___.   2. Roberto likes _____.

3. Roberto likes ___game___.   4. Silvia likes _____.

5. Silvia likes ___music___.   6. Silvia likes _____.

7. They both like _____.   8. They both like _____.

9. They both like _____.

C. **Study the chart with your classmates and teacher.**

Simple Present: *Like*			
Subject	**Verb**	**Noun**	**Example sentence**
I, You, We, They	like	movies, music, sports, games, computers, TV, books, restaurants, parks	I **like** computers. You **like** games. We **like** music. They **like** books.
He, She, It	likes		He **likes** parks. She **likes** restaurants.

D. **Complete the sentences with the correct form of *like*.**

1. Antonio _____ *like* _____ computers.
2. Rebecca _____ *like* _____ parks.
3. Antonio and Rebecca _____ *like* _____ movies.
4. We _____ *like* _____ games.
5. The students _____ *like* _____ books.
6. I _____.

E. **COMPARE AND CONTRAST** **Read the Venn diagram about Roberto's children.**

Carla likes ...
restaurants
books
_____
_____
_____

Carla and Juan like ...
movies
music
_____
_____
_____

Juan likes ...
sports
computers
_____
_____
_____

F. Create sentences and repeat them to a partner.

1. _Carla likes restaurants_ _____ .

2. _____ .

3. _____ .

4. _____ .

G. **CLASSIFY** Write Silvia's and Roberto's information from Exercise A into the Venn diagram.

Roberto

Roberto and Silvia

Silvia

H. **COMPARE AND CONTRAST** Talk to a partner and complete the diagram. Ask: *What things do you like?*

I like ...

I like tea, T.v
I like cooking
I like Restuaent

We both like ...

My partner likes ...

Hosefa
My foiend Meeta
she like sing sliping
she like speeking
He like banana
she like T.v
she like shopping
she like music
she like Runing
she like Cooking

I. Introduce your partner to your classmates.

EXAMPLE: This is my friend Roberto. He is from Mexico. He is married and has two children. Roberto likes movies and books.

LESSON **5** When do you study?

GOAL ■ Plan a schedule

A. INTERPRET Complete the information about what Roberto does.

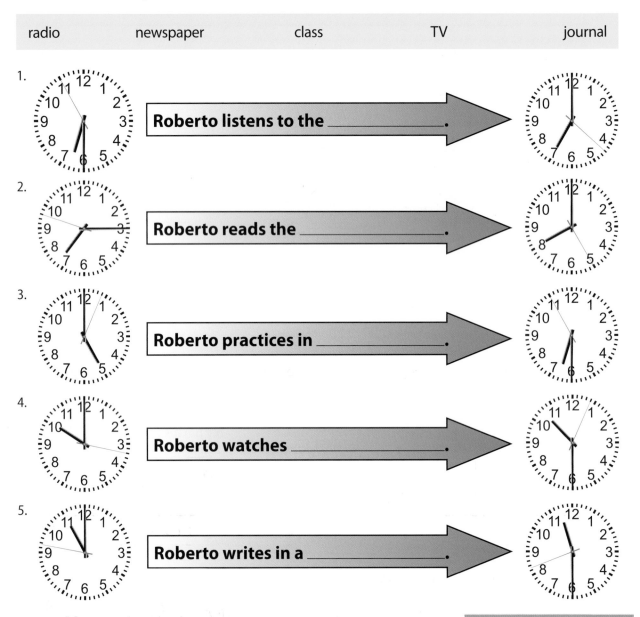

| radio | newspaper | class | TV | journal |

1. Roberto listens to the _____.

2. Roberto reads the _____.

3. Roberto practices in _____.

4. Roberto watches _____.

5. Roberto writes in a _____.

B. Complete the sentences about Roberto's schedule.

START	FINISH
from 3:00	to 10:00

1. He reads the newspaper from ____7:15____ to ____8.00____.

2. He practices English in class from _____ to _____.

3. He watches TV from _____ to _____.

4. He writes in a journal from _____ to _____.

26 Unit 1

C. Look at the clocks. Write the times.

1. Lidia reads the newspaper at
___6:45___.

2. Lidia listens to the radio at
_____.

3. Lidia practices English in class at
_____.

4. Lidia writes in a journal at
_____.

D. Write Lidia's schedule.

Time	Activity
6:45	She reads the newspaper.

E. Listen and write Juan's schedule.

CD 1
TR 22

Start time	End time	Activity
6:00	6:30	Juan eats breakfast.
		Juan reads the newspaper.
		Juan listens to the radio.
		Juan writes in a journal.
		Juan practices English in class.

F. Write sentences about Juan's schedule.

1. Juan ___eats breakfast___ from ___6:00___ to ___6:30___.
2. Juan _____ from _____ to _____.
3. Juan _____ from _____ to _____.
4. Juan _____ from _____ to _____.
5. Juan _____ from _____ to _____.

G. Write your schedule in the chart.

	Start time	End time	Activity
in the morning			
in the afternoon			
at night			

H. Talk to a partner. Ask: *When do you practice English?* Write the schedule in the chart.

	Start time	End time	Activity
in the morning			
in the afternoon			
at night			

I. Report the information about your partner to a group.

Before You Watch

A. **Look at the picture. Complete the sentences.**

1. Picture 1 shows

   _____.

2. In picture 2, we see a

   _____.

3. The boy in picture 3 is a

   _____.

While You Watch

B. ▶ **Watch the video. Complete the dialog.**

Naomi: Nice to meet you, too, Mrs. Sanchez. Hector was showing me some of the
(1) _____ family _____ photos.

Mrs. Sanchez: Oh, was he? Well, this is my (2) _____. She's married, and she has two kids.

Naomi: So, these are your (3) _____?

Hector: Yes, (4) _____ and Marta.

Mrs. Sanchez: Aiden is 10, and Marta is 8. Aren't they (5) _____? Oh, and this is my brother, and these are my parents. They all live in New York.

Hector: (6) _____, take it easy! Naomi doesn't need to know our whole family history.

Check Your Understanding

C. **Read the statements. Write *T* for True and *F* for False.**

1. Hector's mother is from Mexico.   ____ F ____

2. Hector's father is 50 years old.   _____

3. Mrs. Sanchez's sister is married.   _____

4. Hector has two cousins named Aidan and Marta.   _____

5. Naomi is from Japan.   _____

Review

Learner Log

I can ask and give personal information.   I can describe people.
☐ Yes ☐ No ☐ Maybe   ☐ Yes ☐ No ☐ Maybe

A.   Complete the chart about Trinh, Duong, and Alan.

Trinh Hong

33 years old
Single
Cambodia

Duong Bui

33 years old
Married
Vietnam

Alan Hart

64 years old
Divorced
United States

Name	Marital status	Age	Country
1. Trinh Hong			
2. Duong Bui			
3. Alan Hart			

B.   Check the correct answer.

1. My name _____ Duong.

   ☐ am   ☐ is   ☐ was

2. I _____ from Vietnam.

   ☐ am   ☐ is   ☐ are

3. Roberto _____ from Mexico.

   ☐ am   ☐ is   ☐ are

4. Roberto and Duong _____ students.

   ☐ am   ☐ is   ☐ are

5. Roberto and Duong _____ black hair.

   ☐ has   ☐ have   ☐ are

6. Roberto _____ one brother.

   ☐ has   ☐ have   ☐ is

7. Silvia _____ 23 years old.

   ☐ has   ☐ have   ☐ is

Learner Log

I can describe my family relationships.	I can express preferences.
■ Yes ■ No ■ Maybe	■ Yes ■ No ■ Maybe

C. Read the sentences and complete Duong's license.

Duong's birth date is July 2, 1979.

His address is 23 South Street.

He lives in New York City, NY.

He is 5'6" tall.

He has brown eyes.

His zip code is 10038.

He is 165 pounds.

DRIVER'S LICENSE

Name:_____

Age:_____ Weight:_____

Height:_____ Eyes:_____

Address:_____

City:_____

State:_____ Zip Code:_____

**D. Match the questions and answers.
Write the correct letter next to each number.**

1. __d__ What's your name?

2. _____ Where are you from?

3. _____ How old are you?

4. _____ What is your weight?

5. _____ How tall are you?

6. _____ Are you married?

a. 6 feet, 2 inches.

b. 28.

c. Yes, I am.

d. Ernesto Gonzalez.

e. 195 pounds.

f. Colombia.

E. What is the relationship? Look at page 21 and fill in the missing words.

1. Silvia is Juan's mother, and Juan is Silvia's _____ *son* _____.

2. Juan is Carla's brother, and Carla is Juan's _____.

3. Roberto is Carla's father, and Carla is Roberto's _____.

4. Roberto and Silvia are Juan and Carla's _____.

5. Juan and Carla are Roberto and Silvia's _____.

F. Unscramble the family words.

1. tehrfa _____ *father* _____

2. nos _____

3. dlehcinr _____

4. htreaudg _____

5. tehrmo _____

G. **What does Silvia like? Fill in the missing words.**

1. She likes ____TV____.

2. She likes _____.

3. She likes the _____.

4. She likes the _____.

H. **How does Roberto practice English? Fill in the missing verbs.**

1. He ____listens____ to
the _____.

2. He _____ the
_____.

3. He _____ the
_____.

4. He _____ in
_____.

I. **What time is it? Write the times.**

1. It's ____11:30____.

2. It's _____.

3. It's _____.

4. It's _____.

J. **Describe two of your classmates.**

John has short black hair and brown eyes. _____

_____

_____

TEAM PROJECT ✓ Create a student profile

In this project, you will work together to create a student profile for one person on your team.

1. **COLLABORATE** Form a team with four or five students. Choose a position for each member of your team.

Position	Job description	Student name
Student 1: **Team Leader**	Check that everyone speaks English. Check that everyone participates.	
Student 2: **Secretary**	Complete the student profile with help from the team.	
Student 3: **Student for profile**	Give personal information for introductions.	
Students 4/5: **Hosts or Hostesses**	Introduce student to other groups.	

2. Create a student profile sheet. Write questions. See page 31 for help.

3. Choose one student in your group to create a profile for.

4. Complete the student profile sheet by asking questions. Each student in the group asks three or more questions.

5. Practice introducing and describing the student to other groups. Use the profile sheet.

6. Create more student profiles if you have time.

EXPLORER GORDON WILTSIE

The Adventure Photographer

"The best tactic for the photographer is to work hard to blend in."
—Gordon Wiltsie

A. PREDICT Answer the questions about Gordon Wiltsie.

1. What is his job?

   a. He is a writer.   b. He is a photographer.   c. He is a skier.

2. Where does he work?

   a. He works in the mountains.   b. He works in the ocean.   c. He works in his house.

3. Where is he from?

   a. He is from California.   b. He is from Europe.   c. He is from Mexico.

B. PREDICT Look at the photograph. What can you say about Gordon?

Name: _____

Age: _____

Height: _____

Marital Status: _____

Country: _____

Eye Color: _____

Hair Color: _____

C. Read the interview with Gordon Wiltsie. Then, check your predictions in Exercise B.

We meet with Gordon Wiltsie, a 63-year-old American photographer.

Interviewer: Gordon, it is great to meet with you. You are tall!

Gordon: Well, I'm 5'11".

Interviewer: We want to ask you a few questions about your work and your life.

Gordon: It is a pleasure. Please ask anything you would like.

Interviewer: Well, first, where are you from?

Gordon: I am from Bishop, California. It is a small town near beautiful mountains.

Interviewer: What do you do?

Gordon: I am a photographer. I go to mountains all over the world and study different cultures and people. I wake up very early in the morning before the sun and work through the day until it is dark.

Interviewer: Are you married?

Gordon: Yes, my wife's name is Meredith.

Interviewer: Well, it sounds like you have a wonderful life.

Gordon: Yes, I do.

D. APPLY Complete the information about you.

Name: _____

Age: _____

Height: _____

Marital Status: _____

Country: _____

Eye Color: _____

Hair Color: _____

Let's Go Shopping

Shoppers walk in the Grand Bazaar in Istanbul, Turkey and look at brightly colored lamps and other things.

UNIT OUTCOMES

☐ Identify types of retail stores

☐ Make purchases and read receipts

☐ Identify articles of clothing

☐ Describe clothing

☐ Describe items in a store

Look at the photo and answer the questions.

1. What do you see in the picture?

2. What are the people doing?

3. How much are the lamps?

GOAL ▪ Identify types of retail stores

A. Read about Van.

Van starts school on Monday. She needs a dictionary, sneakers, new blouses, a digital music player, and food for lunches.

B. CLASSIFY Where can Van buy the items? Write the items from Exercise A under the stores below.

dictionary

C. **DEBATE** In a group, discuss the best place to buy each item in your neighborhood.

D. What other things can you buy at each store? Make a list with a group.

_____   _____

_____   _____

_____   _____

CD 1
TR 23
E. **PREDICT** First, predict where Van buys the products. Then, listen and circle the correct place.

Product	Type of Store	
1. a radio	a department store	a convenience store
2. sneakers	a shoe store	a department store
3. shirts	a clothing store	a department store
4. a dictionary	a bookstore	a department store
5. bread, cheese, and fruit	a supermarket	a convenience store

STRESS AND INTONATION

➤ WHERE do VAN // and her HUSband // SHOP for a RADio?

➤ At a dePARTment store.

F. Practice pronouncing the sentences with a partner.

1. Van // shops at the department store // every Wednesday.

2. Her husband // likes to buy food // at the supermarket.

3. Where's // the convenience store?

4. The bookstore // has dictionaries.

G. Use the information in Exercise E to practice the conversation. Use *shoes, shirts, a dictionary,* and *bread, cheese,* and *fruit* in new conversations.

Student A: Where do Van and her husband shop for <u>a radio</u>?
Student B: <u>At a department store.</u>

H. Study the chart with your classmates and teacher.

Simple Present: *Shop*		
Subject	**Verb**	**Example sentence**
I, You, We, They	shop	I **shop** for shoes at a department store. You **shop** for bread at a convenience store. We **shop** for food at a supermarket. They **shop** for books at a bookstore.
He, She, It	shops	He **shops** for shoes at a shoe store. She **shops** for dresses at a clothing store.

I. Complete the sentences with the correct form of *shop*.

1. Van _____*shops*_____ for a radio at a department store.

2. They _____ for food at a supermarket.

3. We _____ for sneakers at a shoe store.

4. He _____ for soda at a convenience store.

5. I _____ for a dictionary at a bookstore.

J. **SURVEY** Make a bar graph. How many of your classmates shop in different types of stores?

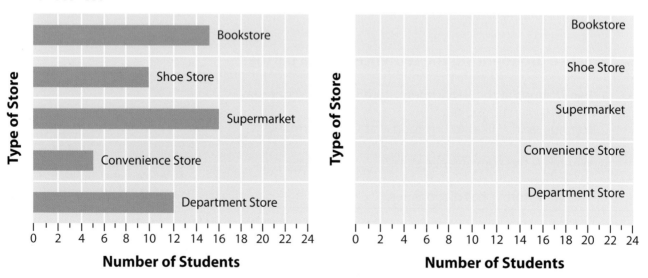

K. Go to a mall or use the Internet. Find the names of three clothing stores that you like. Report them to the class.

LESSON 2 Van's purchases

GOAL ■ Make purchases and read receipts

A. INTERPRET Look at the receipts. What are the totals? What is the tax?

Martin's Department Store

Date: 09-06-2015

Shirt .... 2@$17.98 -	$35.96
Sneakers	$22.99
Subtotal............................	$58.95
Tax....................................	$4.72
TOTAL	$63.67

Customer Copy

HERO BOOKS

Date: 09-06-2015

Bilingual dictionary...........	$21.95
Subtotal............................	$21.95
Tax....................................	$1.76
TOTAL	$23.71

No Returns Without Receipt

Sam's Food Mart

Date: 09-06-2015

Bread...............................	$2.30
Cheese	$2. 75
Oranges @.99 a pound.........	$1.98
Potato Chips	$2. 60
TOTAL	$9.63

THANK YOU for shopping at Sam's.

B. How much is the total for the shirts, sneakers, bilingual dictionary, and food?

$63.67 (clothes) + $23.71 (dictionary) + $ 9.63 (food) = _____

C. Listen and circle the amounts you hear.

CD 1 TR 24

EXAMPLE: $12.50 $2.15   (\$22.50) $22.15

1. $12.95 $34.15 $34.50 $45.50

2. $13.00 $30.00 $33.00 $43.00

3. $ .57 $57.00 $15.70 $17.00

4. $19.75 $17.90 $79.00 $77.95

D. Listen and write the prices.

CD 1 TR 25

Lang's DEPARTMENT STORE

VACUUM	WASHING MACHINE	CANDY BARS	PAPER	CELL PHONE
$ ☐1	$ ☐2	$ ☐3	$ ☐4	$ ☐5

E. **Practice asking about prices. Look at Exercise D on page 41 for information.**

Student A: Excuse me, how much is the <u>vacuum</u>?
Student B: $98.99.
Student C: Thank you.

F. **Write the words from the box under the pictures.**

a nickel	a ten-dollar bill	a penny	a one-dollar bill
a twenty-dollar bill	a quarter	a five-dollar bill	a dime

1. _____ 2. _____ 3. _____ 4. _____

5. _____ 6. _____

7. _____ 8. _____

G. **CALCULATE** **What bills and coins do you need for these items? Tell a partner.**

$53.99 $75.50 $23.71

Bills: _____   Bills: _____   Bills: _____

Coins: _____   Coins: _____   Coins: _____

H. **INTERPRET** **Read the check.**

What is the account holder's name and address?

What is the date?

How much is the check for?

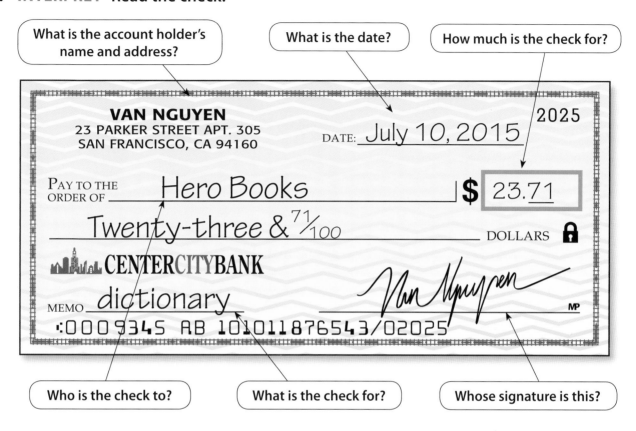

Who is the check to?

What is the check for?

Whose signature is this?

I. Look at the items in Exercises D and G. Which items do you want to buy? Write a check for one of the items.

J. **INVESTIGATE** Visit some banks or use the internet. Find out how to open a checking account.

LESSON ③ Buying new clothes

A. INTERPRET Write the correct letter under each type of clothing. Then, listen for the missing prices.

CD 1
TR 26

a. suit
b. T-shirt
c. ties
d. hat
e. sweater
f. dress
g. socks
h. baseball cap
i. sneakers
j. blouse
k. coat
l. skirt

B. CLASSIFY In a group, write clothing words from Exercise A in the chart. Add other clothing words that you know.

Women's	Men's	Both

C. Study the charts with your classmates and teacher.

Be Verb (Questions)			
Question words	*Be*	**Singular or plural noun**	**Example question**
How much (money)	is	the dress the suit	How much **is** the dress? How much **is** the suit?
How much (money)	are	the socks the ties	How much **are** the socks? How much **are** the ties?

Be Verb (Answers)		
Singular or plural noun or pronoun	*Be*	**Example answer**
It	is	It **is** $48. It's $48. (The dress **is** $48.) It **is** $285. It's $285. (The suit **is** $285.)
They	are	They **are** $12. They're $12. (The socks **are** $12.) They **are** $22. They're $22. (The ties **are** $22.)

D. Practice the conversation.

Student A: How much <u>is the dress</u>?
Student B: <u>It's $48</u>.

E. Ask a partner about the prices. Use the conversation in Exercise D.

Student A asks Student B:

$ _____48_____

$ _____

$ _____

Student B asks Student A:

$ _____

$ _____

$ _____

F. Look at the picture. Where is Gabriela? What is her problem?

G. **INFER** Read about Gabriela. What is her problem?

> Gabriela shops at Dress for Less. It is a clothing store on Main Street. The prices are good, but she only has $75. She needs clothes for a party. She needs a new shirt, a skirt, and a hat. She has a problem.

H. Circle *Yes* or *No*. Look at page 44 for prices.

1. Gabriela shops at Lang's department store.	Yes	No
2. Gabriela has $75.	Yes	No
3. Gabriela can buy a shirt, a skirt, and a hat.	Yes	No

I. Look at the ad on page 44. You have $75. What different items can you buy? Write the items and their prices. Then, talk in a group.

_____   _____   _____

_____   _____   _____

J. **INVESTIGATE** Research clothing stores on the Internet. What can you buy for $100?

LESSON 4 What color is your shirt?

GOAL ■ Describe clothing

CD 1
TR 27

A. Listen and point to the clothing you hear about in the conversation.

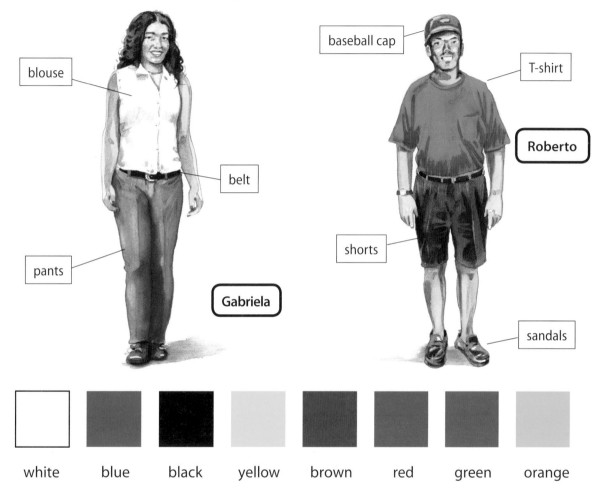

blouse

belt

pants

Gabriela

baseball cap

T-shirt

Roberto

shorts

sandals

| white | blue | black | yellow | brown | red | green | orange |

B. CLASSIFY Complete the chart with the words from the picture. Then, add more clothing words.

Singular	Plural
T-shirt	T-shirts

Plural only

C. Study the chart. Complete the chart with words from the box.

His	Her
My	Our
Your	Their

Pronoun	Possessive Adjectives
I	_____My_____ shirt is blue. _____ shoes are black.
You	_____ baseball cap is blue. _____ shorts are brown.
He	_____ belt is black. _____ sandals are brown.
She	_____ blouse is pink. _____ shoes are white.
We	_____ shirts are white. _____ pants are blue.
They	_____ dresses are red. _____ shoes are black.

D. Look at page 47. Answer the questions.

1. What color are Roberto's shorts?
   His shorts are brown.

2. What color is Gabriela's blouse?

3. What color are Gabriela and Roberto's belts?

4. What color are Gabriela's pants?

5. What color is Roberto's T-shirt?

6. What color are Gabriela and Roberto's shoes?

E. COMPARE AND CONTRAST Talk to a partner and describe your classmates' clothes. Then, write sentences.

My	His
My shirt is _____.	His shirt is _____.
My shoes are _____.	_____
My _____.	_____
_____	_____
_____	_____

Your	Her
Your shirt is _____.	Her shirt is _____.
_____	_____
_____	_____
_____	_____
_____	_____

Our	Their
Our shirts are _____.	Their _____.
_____	_____
_____	_____
_____	_____
_____	_____

F. With a different partner, describe your classmates by their clothes. Let your partner guess who the classmates are.

Student A: Her blouse is blue.
Student B: Amy?

G. CLASSIFY Look around the classroom. In groups, make a list of clothes by color.

Red	Blue	Green	Orange
Carolina's sweater			

LESSON **5** A large TV or a small TV?

GOAL ■ Describe items in a store

A. Look at the pictures. Write a word under each picture.

1. Do you want a small laptop or a large desktop computer?

small
_____

large
_____

2. Do you want a new house or an old house?

_____

_____

3. Do you want a new car or a used car?

_____

_____

4. Do you want a striped shirt or a plaid shirt?

_____

_____

5. Do you want a large blouse or a medium blouse?

_____

_____

6. Do you want a small T-shirt or a medium T-shirt?

_____

_____

B. CLASSIFY Complete the chart. Write the new words from Exercise A.

Size	Age	Pattern
large	used	striped

C. Look at the picture. Where is Tatsuya? What does he want?

CD 1
TR 28

D. Listen to the conversation with your books closed. What does Tatsuya want to buy?

Tatsuya:	Excuse me. I want a <u>TV</u>.
Salesperson:	<u>A **big** TV</u> or <u>a **small** TV</u>?
Tatsuya:	I want <u>a **small** TV</u>.
Salesperson:	OK, how about this one?
Tatsuya:	Yes, that's good. How much is it?
Salesperson:	It's <u>$135</u>.
Tatsuya:	I'll take it!

> **STRESS**
> I want a **SMALL** TV.

E. Practice the conversation with a partner.

F. Practice new conversations. Use the information below. Use the conversation in Exercise D as an example.

Student A is the customer.
Student B is the salesperson.

1. blouse:	medium/small	$24
2. laptops:	large/small	$899
3. refrigerator:	new/used	$210
4. shirt:	small/medium	$18

Student B is the customer.
Student A is the salesperson.

1. car:	used/new	$12,000
2. house:	old/new	$300,000
3. sweater:	striped/ plaid	$42
4. dress:	large/medium	$33

G. **Study the chart with your classmates and teacher.**

Simple Present: *Want*		
Subject	**Verb**	**Example sentence**
I, You, We, They	want	I **want** a large TV.
He, She, It	wants	He **wants** a new house.

CD 1
TR 29-32

H. **Listen to the conversations and circle the correct answers.**

1.
         a small TV   a large TV   a new TV

2.
         a new house   an old house   a small house

3.
         a small blouse   a medium blouse   a large blouse

4.
         a new car   an old car   a used car

I. **Complete the sentences with the correct form of *want*. Use the information from Exercise H.**

1. Tatsuya _____ a small TV.

2. Emily and Steve _____.

3. Gabriela _____.

4. Ivan and Natasha _____.

J. **With a partner, write a conversation like the ones you heard in Exercise H. Present it to the class.**

 # Can I help you?

Before You Watch

A. **PREDICT** Look at the picture. Complete each sentence.

1. Hector is talking to

   _____.

2. They are in a(n)

   _____.

3. Hector is holding a

   _____.

While You Watch

B. ▶ Watch the video. Read the statements. Write *T* for True or *F* for False.

1. A customer comes to the store.   _T_

2. The customer wants a dress.   _____

3. The customer sees three pairs of jeans.   _____

4. The green sweater is the cheapest.   _____

5. The customer is happy.   _____

6. Hector helps the customer.   _____

Check Your Understanding

C. **Put the sentences in order to make a conversation.**

a. _____ **Sales Clerk:** Please follow me to the men's department.

b. _____ **Customer:** I'm looking for a sweater.

c. _1_ **Sales Clerk:** Can I help you?

d. _____ **Customer:** No, it's for my brother.

e. _____ **Sales Clerk:** Is the sweater for you?

f. _____ **Customer:** Thank you.

g. _____ **Sales Clerk:** You're welcome.

A. Listen and write the prices in Column 1.

CD 1
TR 33

Item	How much is it?	Where can you buy it?	Describe it.
		department store	black and white
	$456.78		

B. Complete Columns 2 and 3 in the table above with your ideas.

C. Look at the receipts. What is the total of all three receipts?

Martin's Department Store		ELECTRONICS SURPLUS		SHOE EMPORIUM	
Date: 09-06-2015		Date: 09-26-2015		Date: 09-26-2015	
Shirt	2@$27.98	Magi big screen TV	$789.55	Black Loafers	$44.95
Subtotal	$55.96	Subtotal	$789.55	Subtotal	$44.95
Tax	$4.48	Tax	$63.16	Tax	$3.60
TOTAL	$60.44	TOTAL	$852.71	TOTAL	$48.55
Customer Copy		Customer Copy		Customer Copy	

D. Write a check for the first receipt.

```
_____                              2026
                              DATE: _____
_____

PAY TO THE
ORDER OF _____| $ [        ]

_____ DOLLARS 🔒

🏙 CENTERCITYBANK

MEMO _____                _____        MP
⑈0009345 AB 10101187654 3/02026
```

E. Write the word under each picture.

1. _____

2. _____

3. _____

F. **Describe the pictures. Use** *his, her,* **or** *their.*

Eva

Duong

1. What color is Eva's hat? Her hat is blue. _____

2. What color is Duong's cap? _____

3. What color is Duong's shirt? _____

4. What color are Eva's pants? _____

5. What color are Eva and Duong's shoes? _____

6. What color is Duong's belt? _____

G. **Write sentences about things you want in Unit 2.**

1. I want a vacuum. _____

2. _____

3. _____

4. _____

5. _____

H. **Talk to a partner. Write sentences about things your partner wants in Unit 2.**

1. Eduardo wants a car. _____

2. _____

3. _____

4. _____

5. _____

✔ **Plan a department store**

In this project, you will plan a department store and present it to the class.

1. **COLLABORATE** Form a team with four or five students. In your team, you need:

Position	Job desciption	Student name
Student 1: **Team Leader**	Check that everyone speaks English. Check that everyone participates.	
Student 2: **Architect**	With help from the team, draw the floor plan.	
Student 3: **Sales Manager**	With help from the team, list the prices of the items in your store.	
Students 4/5: **Writers**	With help from the team, prepare a role-play to present to the class.	

2. Choose a name for your department store.

   _____

3. Draw a floor plan of your store in your notebook.

4. Make a list of ten things you sell. Include their prices. Where are the items located on your floor plan?

   _____   _____

   _____   _____

   _____   _____

   _____   _____

5. Prepare a role-play in which a person in your group talks to a salesperson and buys some things. You can also make checks and receipts. Students in your group can take on the roles of a salesperson, a cashier, a customer or customers, and a manager.

6. Practice the role-play and present it to the class.

EXPLORER ANDREW SKURKA

Relationships With Nature

"Relationships are the most important things in life, specifically relationships with nature, others, and self."
—Andrew Skurka

A. Complete Column 1. Make a list of the clothing Andrew is wearing in the picture.

Clothing	Types of Stores

B. PREDICT Where do you think Andrew shops for the clothing? Complete Column 2 in Exercise A.

C. Read about Andrew.

> National Geographic Explorer Andrew Skurka is a speaker and an author. He is also an adventurer and a guide. He is the author of a book for campers and hikers. Campers stay in one place and hikers walk from one place to another. Campers need different clothing than hikers.
>
> Before a trip, Andrew goes shopping for important items. He shops for hiking boots at the shoe store. He shops for sweaters, shirts, and pants at the clothing store or the department store. Sometimes he shops at sporting goods stores for clothing, too. Andrew travels for a long time, so he also shops for a few interesting books to read at the bookstore.

D. What are Andrew's four jobs?

_____   _____   _____   _____

E. ANALYZE Look at the list of clothing and supplies. Write *speaker, author, adventurer,* or *guide* next to each item. You can write more than one job next to the items.

Clothing	Andrew's Job
boots	*adventurer / guide*
cap or hat	
computer	
dictionary	
jacket or coat	
paper	
suit	
sunglasses	
tent	

F. APPLY What do you need for school or work? Make a list with a partner.

_____   _____

_____   _____

_____   _____

Food

People walk and buy
their food in a busy
food market.

UNIT OUTCOMES

☐ Identify common meals and foods

☐ Interpret food advertisements

☐ Express needs

☐ Compare prices

☐ Take and place orders

Look at the photo and answer the questions.

1. What do you see in the photo?

2. Where are the people?

3. What are the people doing?

LESSON ❶ What's for lunch?

GOAL Identify common meals and foods

A. Look at the photo. Where is Dave? What food will he eat? Then, read about Dave.

I'm Dave Chen. I'm an English teacher in Florida. I like to eat! I eat a big breakfast in the morning at around seven, a small lunch at noon, and a big dinner at about six o'clock.

B. Practice the conversation.

Mario: Dave, what time do you eat <u>breakfast?</u>

Dave: Oh, at about <u>7:00 a.m.</u> How about you, Mario?

Mario: I eat breakfast at <u>8:00 a.m.</u>

C. **SURVEY** Ask four students: *What time do you eat breakfast, lunch, and dinner?*

Name	Breakfast	Lunch	Dinner
Dave	7:00 a.m.	12:00 p.m.	6:00 p.m.
You			

D. Read the foods in the box with your classmates and teacher.

a hamburger	spaghetti	toast	french fries	cereal
a sandwich	roast beef	eggs	fried chicken	

E. **PREDICT AND CLASSIFY** What do you think Dave eats for breakfast, lunch, and dinner? Complete the diagram with the foods from the box.

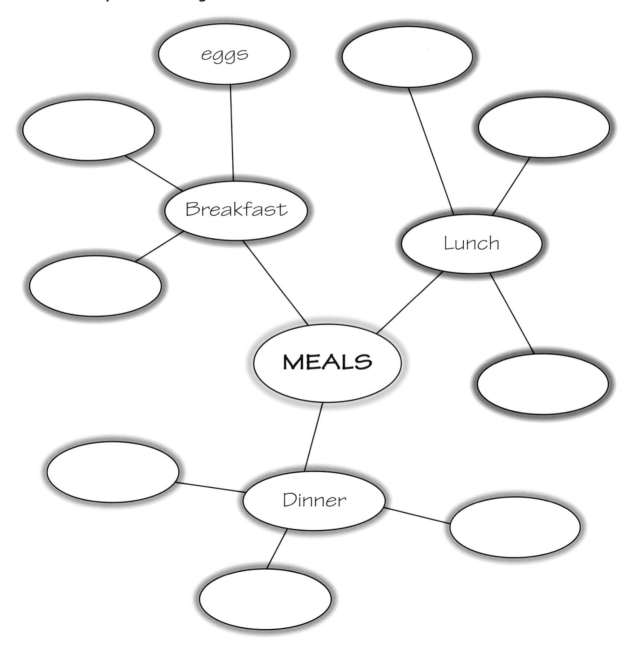

F. Listen to Dave and check the information in Exercise E.

CD 1
TR 34

G. Practice the conversation. Make new conversations with the food words.

Mario: What do you like for lunch?
Jim: I like <u>egg rolls</u>. How about you?
Mario: I like <u>tacos</u>.

roast beef and potatoes

rice and beans

pasta

egg rolls

H. Practice in groups of four or five.

Student A: What do you like for lunch?
Student B: I like hamburgers.
Student C: He likes hamburgers, and I like sandwiches.
Student D: He likes hamburgers, she likes sandwiches, and I like soup.

> **SIMPLE PRESENT**
> I like . . .
> He/She likes . . .

I. **CLASSIFY** What do you eat for breakfast, lunch, and dinner?

Breakfast	Lunch	Dinner

J. **APPLY** Write sentences about what you like for breakfast, lunch, and dinner.

1. I like _____ for breakfast.

2. _____ for lunch.

3. _____.

GOAL ■ Interpret food advertisements

A. INTERPRET Read the advertisement with your classmates and teacher.

B. Listen to Duong and his wife make a shopping list. What do they need to buy? Check *Yes* or *No*.

CD 1
TR 35

Do they need . . .	Yes	No
ground beef?		
spaghetti?		
milk?		
carrots?		
tomatoes?		
peanut butter?		
soda?		
avocados?		

C. Write sentences about what Duong and Minh need.

1. *They need ground beef.*

2. _____

3. _____

D. INTERPRET Study the advertisement with your classmates and teacher.

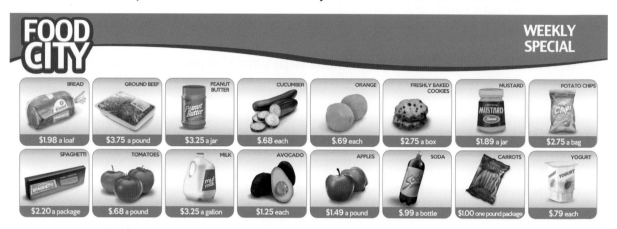

E. ANALYZE Scan the advertisement. Complete the chart with information from Exercise D.

Product	Container or Quantity	Price
cookies		$2.75
	bag	$2.75
		$.99
	each	
	each	
	each	$1.25
	each	$.68
		$3.25
	jar	$1.89
peanut butter		
	loaf	
	package	$2.20
		$1.00
tomatoes		
	pound	
	pound	$3.75

F. Read the chart.

Be Verb	
How much **is** the	bread? peanut butter?
How much **are** the	tomatoes? potato chips?

G. Practice the conversation. Student A asks questions. Student B looks at the advertisement on page 66 to answer. Ask about *peanut butter, tomatoes, milk,* and *cookies.*

Student A:	How much is the peanut butter?	**Student A:**	How much are the tomatoes?
Student B:	It's $3.25 a jar.	**Student B:**	They are $.68 a pound.

H. Practice the conversation. Student B asks questions. Student A looks at the advertisement on page 66 to answer. Ask about *bread, potato chips, soda,* and *apples.*

Student A:	How much is the bread?	**Student A:**	How much are the potato chips?
Student B:	It's $1.98 a loaf.	**Student B:**	They are $2.75 a bag.

I. DESIGN In a group, make your own food advertisement.

News Observer   Sunday, October 1

J. Look at a food advertisement in a local newspaper or search on an online store. Are the prices in your advertisement in Exercise I more expensive or cheaper?

LESSON ③ What do we need?

GOAL ■ Express needs

A. INTERPRET Look at the picture. Where is Doung? What is Doung eating? Then, read Duong's story.

> EAT OUT
> eat out = eat at a restaurant

> My name is Duong. I'm from Vietnam. I study at North Creek Adult School. It is very expensive to eat out every day, so I bring my lunch to school. My wife and I go to the store every Saturday. We buy bread and meat for my sandwiches.

B. Answer the questions. Check (✓) *True* or *False*.

	True	False
1. Duong buys his lunch at school.	☐	☐
2. Duong and his son go to the store every Saturday.	☐	☐
3. Duong and his wife buy bread and meat for sandwiches.	☐	☐

C. Listen to the conversation between Duong and Minh. Check (✓) the foods they need from the supermarket.

CD 1
TR 36

Shopping List

_____ ham	_____ turkey
_____ tuna fish	_____ chicken
_____ peanut butter	_____ salami
_____ jelly	

D. Study the words for food containers. Write the correct word under each picture.

bag	bottle	~~can~~	jar	box	package

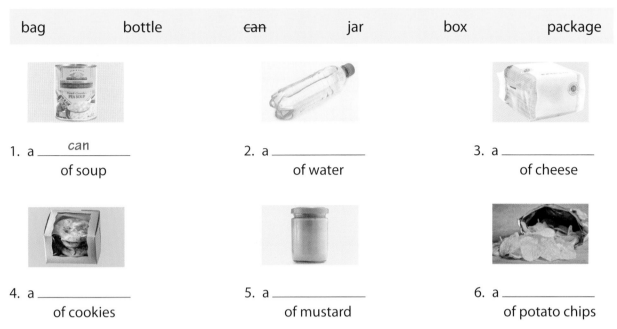

1. a ___can___ of soup

2. a _____ of water

3. a _____ of cheese

4. a _____ of cookies

5. a _____ of mustard

6. a _____ of potato chips

E. In a group, discuss what other foods go into each container.

Container	Food
can / cans	beans, coffee
bottle / bottles	
package / packages	
box / boxes	
jar / jars	
bag / bags	

PLURALS

/z/	/iz/
jar**z**	packag**iz**
bag**z**	box**iz**
can**z**	

F. Create sentences by adding words from Exercise E. Then, read your sentences to a partner.

1. Alicia needs three cans of _____ coffee _____.

2. She needs four bottles of _____.

3. She needs two packages of _____.

4. _____ three boxes of _____.

5. _____.

6. _____.

G. Study the chart with your classmates and teacher.

Simple Present		
Subject	**Verb**	**Example sentence**
I, You, We, They	eat like need want make	I **eat** tacos for lunch. You **like** eggs for breakfast. We **need** three cans of corn. They **want** three boxes of cookies. I **make** sandwiches for lunch.
He, She, It	eats likes needs wants makes	He **eats** pizza for dinner. She **likes** tomato soup. He **needs** three pounds of tomatoes. She **wants** two bottles of water. She **makes** sandwiches for Duong.

H. Read the shopping list.

Shopping List

6 bottles of water

3 cans of soup

1 jar of jelly

3 packages of cheese

I. Complete the sentences with the correct form of the verbs in parentheses and the correct containers.

1. Duong _____needs_____ (need) one _____jar_____ of jelly.

2. They _____ (like) soup at night.

3. Duong _____ (eat) sandwiches at school.

4. Minh _____ (make) sandwiches for Duong.

5. They _____ (want) three _____ of cheese.

J. Make a list of things you need at the store. Tell your partner what you need.

GOAL ■ Compare prices

A. EVALUATE Look at Duong's shopping list. Look at the advertisement on page 65 for Puente Market and the advertisement on page 66 for Food City. Which store is cheaper for Duong?

Shopping List

2 pounds of ground beef

3 pounds of tomatoes

avocados

carrots

B. Study the graph. Fill in the missing information.

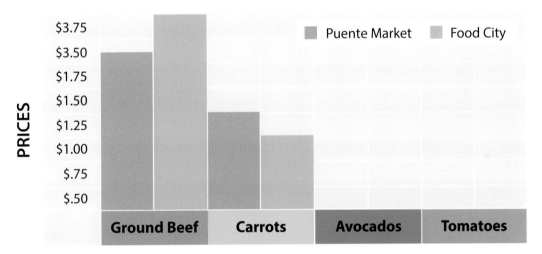

C. Complete the chart and calculate the totals.

	Puente Market	Food City
Ground beef	$3.40	$3.75
Carrots		
Avocados		
Tomatoes		
Total		

D. Study the charts with your classmates and teacher.

Cheaper		
	Question	**Answer**
Singular	Where is ground beef cheaper?	It's **cheaper** at Puente Market.
Plural	Where are carrots cheaper?	They're **cheaper** at Food City.

More Expensive		
	Question	**Answer**
Singular	Where is ground beef more expensive?	It's **more expensive** at Food City.
Plural	Where are carrots more expensive?	They're **more expensive** at Puente Market.

E. Practice the conversation. Make new conversations comparing prices. Use the prices on page 71.

> **STRESS**
>
> **WHERE** is ground **beef CHEAPER**?
> **WHERE** is ground **beef** more **EXPENSIVE**?
>
> **WHERE** are **carrots CHEAPER**?
> **WHERE** are **carrots** more **EXPENSIVE**?

Student A: I need some ground beef. Where is it cheaper?
Student B: It's cheaper at Puente Market.

F. Practice the conversation. Make new conversations comparing prices. Use the prices on page 71.

Student A: I buy ground beef at Puente Market.
Student B: Why?
Student A: It's more expensive at Food City.

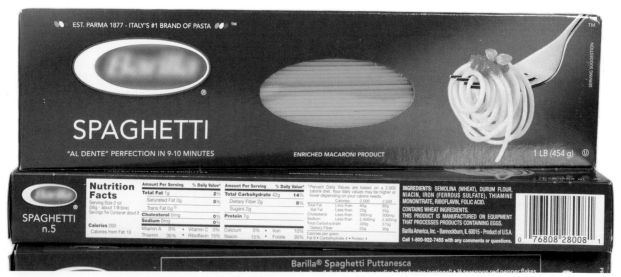

G. **INTERPRET** Read the paragraph about Sebastian.

> I shop at Food City. I like the bananas and oranges there. The fruit is more expensive, but I like the store. They have good specials, too. Food City is near my home.

H. **Answer the questions. Check (✓) *True* or *False*.**

	True	False
1. Sebastian shops at Puente Market.	☐	☐
2. The fruit at Puente Market is cheaper.	☐	☐
3. Food City has bananas and oranges.	☐	☐

I. **COMPARE** Listen to Sebastian ask about prices. Complete the charts.

CD 1
TR 37

Puente Market	
Fruit	**Price**
bananas	$.92
oranges	
pears	
apples	

Food City	
Fruit	**Price**
bananas	$.98
oranges	
pears	
apples	

J. **CREATE** Complete the bar graph about the two markets. Use the information from Exercise I.

	Puente Market	Food City	Puente Market	Food City	Puente Market	Food City	Puente Market	Food City
$2.50								
$2.00								
$1.75								
$1.50								
$1.25								
$1.00								
$ .75								
	bananas		oranges		pears		apples	

K. **APPLY** What store do you shop at? Why? Tell the group.

L. As a class, choose one food item. Choose two stores in your neighborhood or go online. Compare prices of the food item. Which store is cheaper?

LESSON **5** **Buying lunch**

GOAL ■ Take and place orders

A. **Study the menu on the lunch truck with your classmates and teacher.**

B. **CLASSIFY** **Write the information from the menu in the chart below.**

Sandwiches	Beverages	Side orders

C. **Practice the conversation. Make new conversations. Change the underlined words.**
Use the words from Exercise B.

Sebastian: Hi! I want a <u>ham sandwich</u>, please.
Server: Do you want a side order?
Sebastian: Yes, a <u>salad</u>.
Server: Great! Do you want a drink?
Sebastian: <u>Milk</u>, thanks.

SINGULAR	PLURAL
a burger	two burger**s**
a salad	three salad**s**
	french frie**s**

D. Look at the menu in Exercise A. Talk to your classmates and teacher. What do you like to eat? What is cheap?

E. Listen to the orders. Write each student's order in the chart below. Write the prices from Exercise A.

CD 1
TR 38-40

1. Manny's order

Selection	Section	Price
soda	beverages	
cheeseburger	sandwiches	
green salad	side orders	
	Total	

2. Tran's order

Selection	Section	Price
	Total	

3. Miyuki's order

Selection	Section	Price
	Total	

F. Study the chart with your classmates and teacher.

Questions and *Yes/No* Answers		
Question	Yes	No
Do you want a hamburger?	Yes, I do.	No, I don't.
Do they want sandwiches?	Yes, they do.	No, they don't.
Does he want a sandwich?	Yes, he does.	No, he doesn't.
Does she want a hot dog?	Yes, she does.	No, she doesn't.

G. Read the orders.

Sebastian
Sandwich: ham sandwich
Side order: salad
Beverage: milk

Tri
Sandwich: cheeseburger
Side order: french fries
Beverage: milk

Natalia
Sandwich: hot dog
Side order: french fries
Beverage: orange juice

H. Answer the questions.

1. Does Sebastian want a salad? _____ *Yes, he does.* _____

2. Does Natalia want orange juice? _____

3. Do Sebastian and Tri want orange juice? _____

4. Do Sebastian and Tri want milk? _____

5. Do Tri and Natalia want ham sandwiches? _____

6. Does Natalia want a cheeseburger? _____

I. Look at the menu on page 74. Write your order. Then, practice taking an order with a partner. Use the conversation in Exercise C as a model.

Selection	Section	Price

J. Go to a lunch truck or cafeteria and order your lunch in English.

LIFESKILLS  Nobody has pizza for breakfast

Before You Watch

A. Look at the picture. Complete each sentence.

1. Hector is holding vegetables and

   _____.

2. It's time for _____.

3. The family is in _____.

While You Watch

B. ▶ Watch the video. Complete the dialog. Use the words in the box.

~~eggs~~	make	milk	sugar	vegetables

Mrs. Sanchez: You should have *real* food for breakfast: (1) _____*eggs*_____, milk, fruit. Please, let me make something for you.

Hector: How about some cake? Cake has eggs and (2) _____ and fruit!

Mrs. Sanchez: It also has sugar in it. Lots and lots of (3) _____. Isn't there anything else in the refrigerator besides pizza and cake?

Hector: There's… Well, there's (4) _____, cheese, and eggs.

Mr. Sanchez: Why don't you (5) _____ an omelet?

Check Your Understanding

C. Watch the video. Read the statements. Write *T* for True or *F* for False.

1. Hector eats pizza for breakfast.   ___F___

2. Mr. Sanchez wants cake for breakfast.   _____

3. Hector takes vegetables out of the refrigerator.   _____

4. Mrs. Sanchez adds milk to the eggs.   _____

5. Hector puts sugar on his omelet.   _____

Review

Learner Log

I can name different foods for different meals.   I can read advertisements.
■Yes ■No ■Maybe   ■Yes ■No ■Maybe

A. Write the names of the foods and drinks in the chart. Are they for breakfast, lunch, or dinner? Add more foods to each list.

Breakfast	Lunch	Dinner

B. Talk to a partner about what he or she eats. Write the information.

1. What do you eat for breakfast? _____

2. What do you eat for lunch? _____

3. What do you eat for dinner? _____

C. Write what you like to eat.

Breakfast	Lunch	Dinner

D. Complete the sentences.

1. I _____ like toast _____ for breakfast.

2. My partner _____ for breakfast.

3. I _____ for lunch.

4. My partner _____ for lunch.

5. I _____ for dinner.

6. My partner _____ for dinner.

Learner Log

I can express needs and quantities.   I can compare prices.
☐ Yes ☐ No ☐ Maybe   ☐ Yes ☐ No ☐ Maybe

E. **Read the advertisement.**

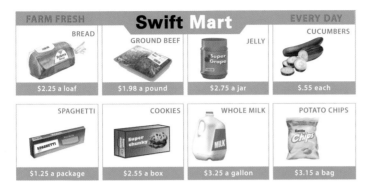

F. **Complete the chart. Use the information from Exercise E.**

Product	Container or Quantity	Price
bread		
ground beef		
jelly		
cucumbers		
spaghetti		
cookies		
milk		
potato chips		

G. **Ask a partner questions about the advertisement in Exercise E. Ask:** *How much is . . .?* **or** *How much are . . .?*

H. **Look at Sebastian's shopping list. What does he need? Write sentences.**

Shopping List
6 bottles of water
1 jar of peanut butter
2 pounds of tomatoes
1 gallon of milk

1. Sebastian _____ six bottles of water.

2. _____

3. _____

4. _____

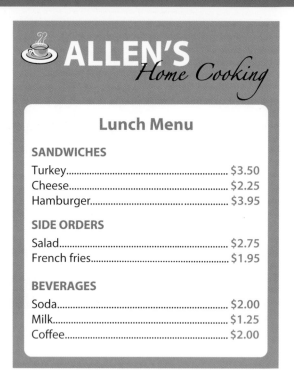

Rudolf's Café

Lunch Menu

SANDWICHES

Ham..$2.75
Tuna...$2.75
Hamburger...................................$3.50

SIDE ORDERS

Salad..$1.98
Soup...$1.75
French fries..................................$1.50

BEVERAGES

Soda...$1.50
Milk..$1.00
Coffee...$1.50

ALLEN'S *Home Cooking*

Lunch Menu

SANDWICHES

Turkey..$3.50
Cheese..$2.25
Hamburger...................................$3.95

SIDE ORDERS

Salad..$2.75
French fries..................................$1.95

BEVERAGES

Soda...$2.00
Milk..$1.25
Coffee...$2.00

I.   Read the menu. Circle _R_ for Rudolf's Café or _A_ for Allen's Home Cooking.

1. Which is cheaper—a hamburger at Rudolf's Café or at Allen's Home Cooking?   R   A

2. Which is more expensive—a salad at Rudolf's or at Allen's?   R   A

3. Which is cheaper—coffee at Rudolf's or at Allen's?   R   A

4. Which is more expensive—soda at Rudolf's or at Allen's?   R   A

J.   Answer the questions about you and a partner.

1. Do you like pizza? _____ _Yes, I do._ _____

2. Do you eat hamburgers? _____

3. Do you eat egg rolls? _____

4. Do you make tuna fish sandwiches? _____

5. Does your partner like pizza? _____

6. Does your partner eat hamburgers? _____

7. Does your partner eat egg rolls? _____

8. Does your partner make tuna fish sandwiches? _____

Create a menu for a new restaurant

In this project, you will create a menu for a new restaurant (including foods and prices) and an advertisement for your restaurant. You will also write a conversation between a server and customers in your restaurant as the server takes their orders.

1. **COLLABORATE** Form a team with four or five students. In your team, you need:

Position	Job description	Student name
Student 1: **Team Leader**	Check that everyone speaks English. Check that everyone participates.	
Student 2: **Advertising Agent**	With help from the team, make an advertisement for your restaurant with a few prices.	
Student 3: **Chef**	With help from the team, write a list of foods for the menu. Design the menu.	
Students 4/5: **Trainers**	With help from the team, write a conversation between a server and customers in a restaurant.	

2. Choose a name for your restaurant.

3. Make a list of foods your restaurant serves.

4. Design a menu.

5. Create an advertisement for your restaurant, giving some prices.

6. Create a conversation.

7. Present your conversation and menu to the class.

8. Compare prices on your menu with prices from other teams' menus.

Eat What You Buy

"Use your power as customer and citizen to demand that the businesses you buy from also stop wasting food."
—Tristram Stuart

A. ANALYZE Study the charts and answer the questions.

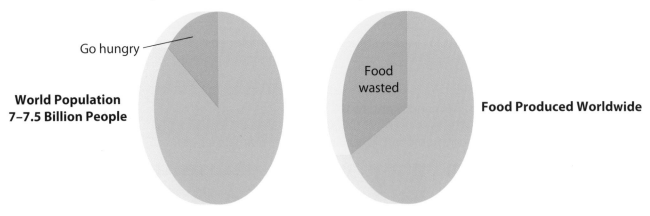

Go hungry

**World Population
7–7.5 Billion People**

Food wasted

Food Produced Worldwide

1. According to the graphs, how many people are in the world? _____

2. According to the graphs, how many people need food but don't have it? _____

3. According to the graphs, what percentage of food is wasted?

   a. one quarter is wasted   b. one third is wasted   c. one half is wasted

B. **PREDICTION** What do you think Tristram Stuart talks about?

C. **Read about Tristram Stuart.**

> Tristram Stuart is an author. He wants people to know that food is important in the world. He says one third of fresh food is wasted every year. Supermarkets don't sell some food because it doesn't look perfect. People throw away food every day, too.
>
> One billion people go hungry every day. Tristram works hard to help people understand that wasting food is very serious. For example, in Portugal, a project called *"Ugly Fruit"* sells fruit that supermarkets don't want. In London and many other places, *"Feeding the 5000"* is a large community party where everyone eats good food that supermarkets don't sell. Tristram wants to help people have food to eat everywhere in the world.

D. **Circle *True* or *False*.**

1. Wasting food is not serious.	True	False
2. 5000 people go hungry every day.	True	False
3. Some supermarkets only sell food that looks perfect.	True	False

E. **CREATE** In a group, create a plan. What comes first? Number the ideas 1–4.

Plan to Avoid Food Waste

_____   Eat leftovers.

___1___   Carefully plan meals.

_____   Go shopping more and buy less food.

_____   Cook only what you need.

F. **APPLY** As a class, add other ideas to avoid waste.

_____

_____

_____

_____

_____

Housing

People in San Francisco call these houses the "painted ladies". They are colorful and make the city look pretty.

UNIT OUTCOMES

☐ Identify types of housing

☐ Describe parts of a home

☐ Interpret classified ads

☐ Use the telephone and make appointments

☐ Identify furniture in a house

Look at the photo and answer the questions.

1. What kind of buildings are in the picture?

2. Do you want to live in a big city?

3. Who lives in these houses?

LESSON ❶ A house or an apartment?

A. INTERPRET Read the web page and underline the information.

1. name of the real estate company

2. phone number

3. name of the salesperson

4. type of housing

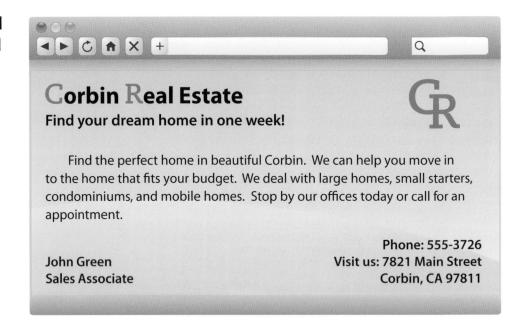

Corbin Real Estate
Find your dream home in one week!

Find the perfect home in beautiful Corbin. We can help you move in to the home that fits your budget. We deal with large homes, small starters, condominiums, and mobile homes. Stop by our offices today or call for an appointment.

John Green
Sales Associate

Phone: 555-3726
Visit us: 7821 Main Street
Corbin, CA 97811

B. INTERPRET Study the pie chart about housing in Corbin. Listen and write the numbers.

CD 1
TR 41

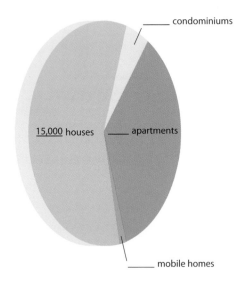

Housing Statistics: Corbin, CA

_____ condominiums

15,000 houses — apartments

_____ mobile homes

C. Complete the chart with the information from Exercise B.

Type of housing	Number of units
Toal number of housing units:	

D. Study the chart with your classmates and teacher.

Simple Present: *Live*		
Subject	**Verb**	**Example sentence**
I, You, We, They	live	I **live** in a house. You **live** in an apartment. We **live** in a condominium. They **live** in a mobile home.
He, She, It	lives	He **lives** in a house. She **lives** in an apartment.

NOTICE

/v/   live

E. Read about the students and their homes.

Saud

Housing: house

Address: 2323 Hartford Rd.

City: Corbin

State: California

Silvia

Housing: mobile home

Address: 13 Palm Ave.

City: Corbin

State: California

Tien

Housing: apartment

Address: 15092 Arbor Lane #22

City: Corbin

State: California

F. Practice the conversation. Then, make new conversations with information from Exercise E.

Saud: Do you live in a house, an apartment, or a condominium?

Tien: I live in <u>an apartment</u>.

Saud: Where do you live?

Tien: My address is <u>15092 Arbor Lane #22</u>.

Saud: Where does Silvia live?

Tien: She lives at <u>13 Palm Ave.</u>

Saud: That's close by.

A /AN

a house

an apartment

G. INTERPRET Read the paragraph.

> Felipe and his sister are from Argentina. Felipe lives in a condominium in Corbin, California. His sister also lives in Corbin. She lives in an apartment. Felipe's brothers live in a small house in Los Angeles. Their parents live in a condominium in Argentina.

H. Write your own paragraph. Use the paragraph in Exercise G as a model. Then, talk with a partner. Write a new paragraph about your partner.

I. SURVEY Ask four classmates what type of housing they live in. Share your information with the class.

Name	Type of housing
Saud	Saud lives in a house.

J. CREATE Combine your information from Exercise I with the rest of the class and create a pie chart.

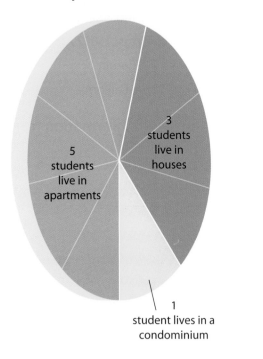

5 students live in apartments

3 students live in houses

1 student lives in a condominium

GOAL   ■ Describe parts of a home

A. **PREDICT** Look at the picture. Where is Saud? Why is he there?

B. Look at the floor plan. Answer the questions.

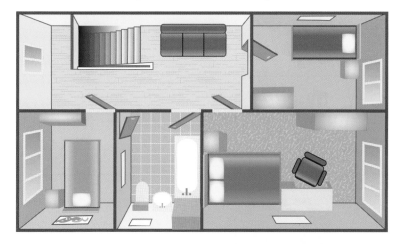

1. How many bedrooms
   are there? _____

2. How many bathrooms
   are there? _____

🎧 **C.** Listen and take notes.
Complete the chart.

CD 1
TR 42-45

Name	Bedrooms	Bathrooms
1. Saud		
2. Silvia		
3. Tien		
4. Felipe		

D. Study the words with your classmates and teacher.

| bedroom | bathroom | kitchen | dining room | living room |

E. Where in a home do people do these things? With a group, write the names of the rooms. Use the words from the box above.

Activity		Room
People sleep in this room.		bedroom
People take showers in this room.		
People watch TV in this room.		
People eat dinner in this room.		
People make dinner in this room.		

F. **IDENTIFY** Practice the conversation. Make new conversations. Talk with a partner.

Student A: Where do people make breakfast?
Student B: People make breakfast in the kitchen.

1. Where do people sleep?
2. Where do people take showers?
3. Where do people watch TV?
4. Where do people eat dinner?
5. Where do people make dinner?

G. Work in groups. Match the letters to the words.

_____ stairs   _____ swimming pool   _____ bathroom   _____ family room

_____ kitchen   _____ garage   _____ hall   _____ balcony

_____ bedroom   _____ deck   _____ front porch   _____ front yard

_____ backyard   _____ driveway

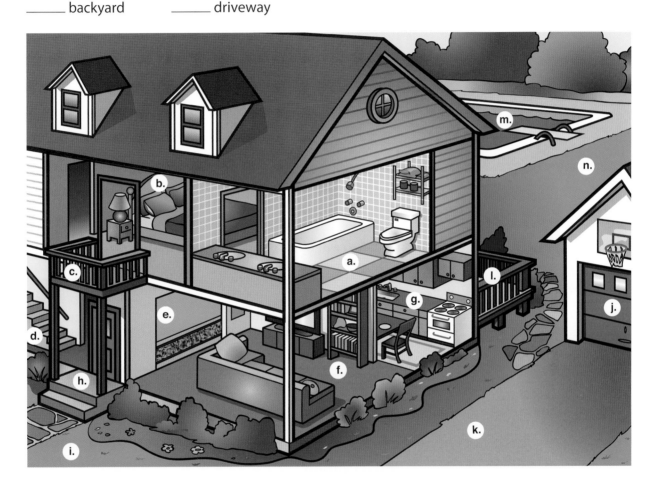

H. APPLY Ask your partner about his or her home. Then, share what you learned with a group.

1. What kind of home do you have?
2. How many bedrooms do you have?
3. How many bathrooms do you have?
4. Do you have a front yard or backyard?
5. Do you have a garage or parking?
6. Do you have a balcony?

HAVE
I **have** . . .
He/She **has** . . .

carport

LESSON ❸ Look in the newspaper

GOAL ▪ Interpret classified ads

A. PREDICT Look at the picture. What is Saud reading? Why?

B. INTERPRET Read the ads and label each *house*, *apartment*, or *condominium*.

a.

AVAILABLE

2 bed, 3 bath condo, nr
schools and parks, gated.
Call 454-7899.

_____

b.

HOME FOR RENT

3 bdrm, 2 bath hse,
Cherry Tree Lane,
a/c, garage, pool,
nice neighborhood, utls pd.,
lease $1, 550. Call 995-5555.

_____

c.

APT. FOR RENT

2br, 2ba apt.,
818 Sundry Cir. #19
2nd fl, furn, balcony.
No pets.
Call 824-7744.

_____

C. Read the classified ads. Write the
abbreviations for bedroom and bathroom
in the chart.

Bedroom	Bathroom

D. Complete the sentences about the
classified ads above with information
about the number of bedrooms and bathrooms.

1. The house *has* _____ bedrooms and _____ bathrooms.

2. The apartment *has* _____.

3. The condominium _____.

4. The house _____ two _____.

E. Read the classified ad and match the word to its abbreviation.

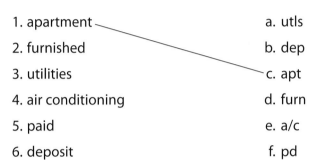

APT. FOR RENT

2 bed, 1 bath apt,
818 Sundry Ave., #13
$900, furn, a/c,
all utls pd, 1 mo dep.
Call 555-6294.

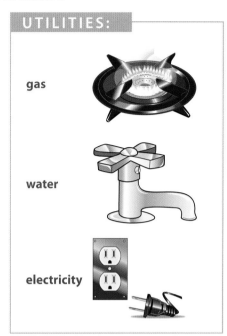

UTILITIES:

gas

water

electricity

1. apartment   a. utls

2. furnished   b. dep

3. utilities   c. apt

4. air conditioning   d. furn

5. paid   e. a/c

6. deposit   f. pd

CD 1
TR 46

F. Read the classified ads. Then, listen and write the letter.

a.

FOR RENT

3 bed, 2 bath apt,
a/c, balcony,
$800. Call Lien
at 555-1734.

b.

APT. FOR RENT

$700/MONTH
1 bed, 1 bath apt.
No pets.
Call Fred at 555-7164.

c.

FOR RENT

2 bed, 3 bath apt.
a/c, elect. pd.
Call Margaret for
more information–
555-2672.

d.

AVAILABLE

3 bed, 3 bath apt.
w/pool, utls pd.,
nr school.
Call 555-5987.

1. _____   2. _____   3. _____   4. _____

G. Study the chart with your classmates and teacher.

Yes/No Questions	
Question	**Answer**
Does it have three bedrooms?	Yes, it does. No, it doesn't.
Does it have air conditioning?	Yes, it does. No, it doesn't.

INTONATION

Yes/No Questions

Does it have three bedrooms?

Does it have air conditioning?

H. **INTERPRET** Read the classified ad and answer the questions.

FOR RENT-CONDO

3 bed, 2 bath condo,
22954 Kensington Place,
a/c, utls pd., lrg yard,
$1,500 a month.
Call Margaret: 555-3452

1. Does the home have four bedrooms? _____

2. Does it have a yard? _____

3. Does it have two bathrooms? _____

4. Does it have furniture? _____

5. Does it have a balcony? _____

I. Put a check (✓) by things in your home. Share the information with a partner.

_____ pets allowed   _____ utilities paid   _____ balcony   _____ garage

_____ air conditioning   _____ near a school   _____ near a park

J. **CREATE** Write a classified ad for your home. Use abbreviations.

K. Look in a newspaper or on the Internet to find a home that is good for you.

LESSON ④ When can I see it?

GOAL ■ Use the telephone and make appointments

A. PREDICT Look at the picture. What is Saud doing? Who is he talking to? Then, read about Saud's plan to find a new home.

Saud's Plan

1. Talk to a rental agent.
2. Read classified ads.
3. Call for appointments.
4. Look at homes.

B. RESEARCH Read different ideas you can use to find a new home.

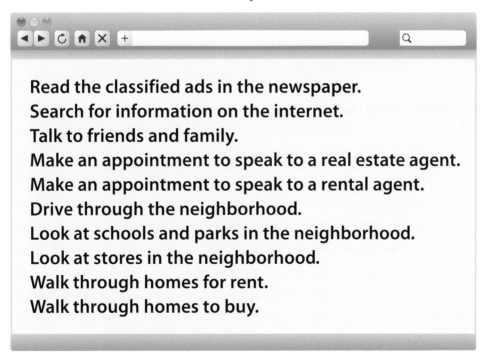

Read the classified ads in the newspaper.
Search for information on the internet.
Talk to friends and family.
Make an appointment to speak to a real estate agent.
Make an appointment to speak to a rental agent.
Drive through the neighborhood.
Look at schools and parks in the neighborhood.
Look at stores in the neighborhood.
Walk through homes for rent.
Walk through homes to buy.

C. CREATE In a group, make a plan to find a new home. Use the ideas from Exercise B.

D. Practice the conversation.

Owner: Hello, can I help you?

Saud: Yes, I am calling about the condominium for rent.

Owner: How can I help you?

Saud: How much is the rent?

Owner: It's $1,200 a month.

Saud: When can I see it?

Owner: How about today at 3:00?

Saud: Great! Thank you.

E. Listen to the conversations. Take notes and complete the chart.

CD 1
TR 47-50

	How much is the rent?	What time is the appointment?
1.	$1,200	3:00
2.		
3.		
4.		

F. Complete Conversation 2 with the information from Exercise E.

Owner: Hello. Can I help you?

Saud: Yes, I am calling about the apartment for rent that I saw in the paper. Is it still available?

Owner: Yes, we are renting it for _____.

Saud: Wow! That sounds expensive.

Owner: Maybe, but it is a beautiful and new apartment.

Saud: OK, when can I see it?

Owner: You can stop by at _____.

G. Practice Conversations 3 and 4 with the information from Exercise E. Use the model in Exercise F.

H. Study the chart with your classmates and teacher.

Present Continuous			
Subject	*Be* **verb**	**Base** + *ing*	**Example sentence**
I	am	talk + *ing*	I **am talking** on the phone.
You, We, They	are	read + *ing* make + *ing*	We **are making** an appointment.
He, She, It	is	move + *ing*	She **is moving** into a new apartment.

I. Write sentences in the present continuous. What is Saud doing?

1. Saud _____ to a rental agent.

2. He _____.

3. He _____.

J. Complete the sentences with the present continuous.

~~read~~	talk	look	move	make

1. I _____ *am reading* _____ the classified ads.

2. They _____ into a new home.

3. We _____ at a condominium.

4. Silvia _____ an appointment.

5. You _____ on the phone.

K. **RANK** In a group, rank the steps from easy to difficult. 1 is easiest.

_____ He talks to a rental agent.   _____ He calls for appointments.

_____ He reads classified ads.   _____ He looks at homes.

LESSON ⑤ Where do you want the sofa?

GOAL ▪ Identify furniture in a house

A. Write the words under the correct room. Share your ideas with a partner.

| bed | car | chair | refrigerator | bathtub | sofa |

1. bedroom _____   2. kitchen _____   3. dining room _____

4. bathroom _____   5. garage _____   6. living room _____

B. CLASSIFY In a group, list the other things you see in the rooms above. Use a dictionary or ask your teacher for help.

Bedroom	Kitchen	Dining room	Bathroom	Garage	Living room

C. Study the prepositions with your classmates and teacher.

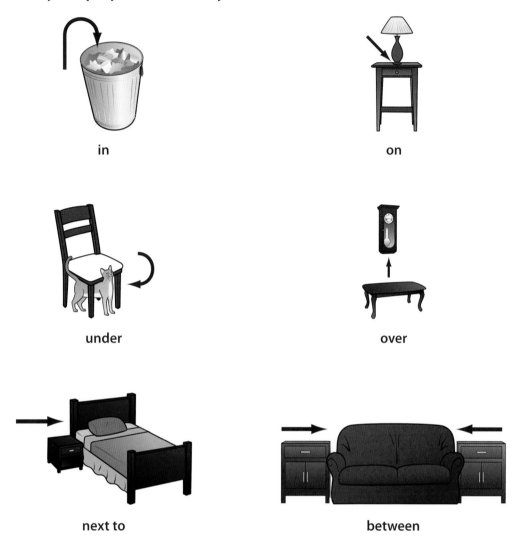

in

on

under

over

next to

between

D. Practice the conversation. Make new conversations. Ask a partner where things are in the pictures above. Ask about *the lamp, the cat, the nightstand, the sofa*, and *the clock*.

Student A: Where's the trash?
Student B: It's in the trash can.

E. Use prepositions to say the location of things in your classroom. Your partner will guess which thing you are talking about.

Student A: It's next to the window.
Student B: The door?

F. Study the words with your classmates and teacher.

a window　　　　　a door　　　　　an end table　　　　　a coffee table

a dining room chair　　　　　a painting　　　　　a lamp

G. Listen to the instructions and add objects to the room below.

CD 1
TR 51

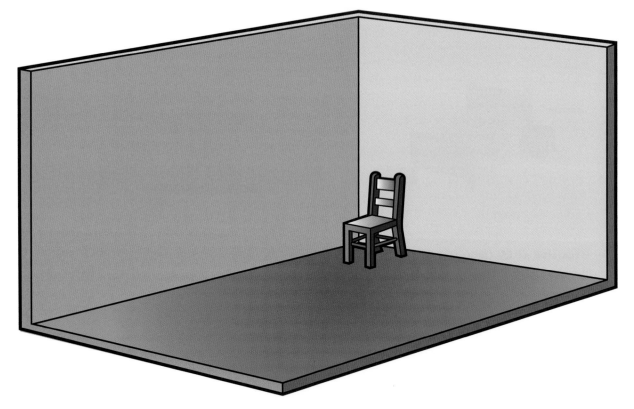

H. **APPLY** Show your partner where the furniture is in your classroom. Walk around the room and talk about it.

I. Find a picture of a room with furniture from a magazine or online. Show the picture to the class and describe it.

Before You Watch

A. **Look at the picture. Complete each sentence.**

1. The sign is for

_____ for rent.

2. The rent is

_____ a month.

3. _____ is

included in the rent.

APARTMENT FOR RENT

$850/month

swimming pool

electricity included

near bus route

call 555-6768

ROUTE 11- BRAND
EXPRESS S

While You Watch

B. ▶ **Watch the video. Complete the dialog. Use the words in the box.**

electricity	garbage	parking	rent	~~utilities~~

Naomi: That's good. What about electricity and water? Are the (1) ___utilities___ included in the rent?

Apartment Manager: Yes, some utilities are included. Water and (2) _____ are included, but you have to pay for the electricity. Do you want to make an appointment to come look at the apartment? It has a very nice view. I'm sure you'll like it.

Naomi: Well… How much is the (3) _____?

Apartment Manager: It's only $900 a month—plus electricity. But the (4) _____ is free!

Naomi: Um, I don't have a car. Well, let's see… $900 a month, plus (5) _____…

Check Your Understanding

C. **Match the questions and answers.**

1. Do you have any apartments for rent?   a. Water is included, but you have to pay for electricity.

2. How much is the rent?   b. Dogs are allowed, but cats aren't.

3. Are the utilities included?   c. Yes, we have two apartments for rent.

4. Do you allow any pets?   d. No, you have to park on the street.

5. Does the building have a garage?   e. The rent is $900 a month.

Review

A. Read the classified ads.

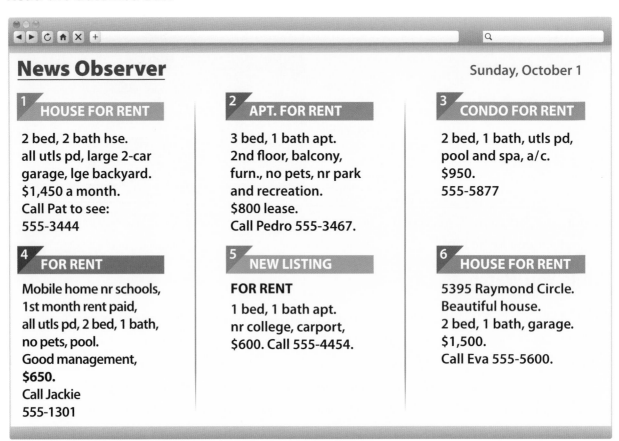

News Observer   Sunday, October 1

1 HOUSE FOR RENT

2 bed, 2 bath hse.
all utls pd, large 2-car
garage, lge backyard.
$1,450 a month.
Call Pat to see:
555-3444

2 APT. FOR RENT

3 bed, 1 bath apt.
2nd floor, balcony,
furn., no pets, nr park
and recreation.
$800 lease.
Call Pedro 555-3467.

3 CONDO FOR RENT

2 bed, 1 bath, utls pd,
pool and spa, a/c.
$950.
555-5877

4 FOR RENT

Mobile home nr schools,
1st month rent paid,
all utls pd, 2 bed, 1 bath,
no pets, pool.
Good management,
$650.
Call Jackie
555-1301

5 NEW LISTING

FOR RENT
1 bed, 1 bath apt.
nr college, carport,
$600. Call 555-4454.

6 HOUSE FOR RENT

5395 Raymond Circle.
Beautiful house.
2 bed, 1 bath, garage.
$1,500.
Call Eva 555-5600.

B. Cover the ads above so you can't see them. Ask your partner questions about the ads and write the information below. Then, your partner covers the ads and asks questions.

What kind of housing is it?	How many bedrooms are there?	How many bathrooms are there?	Is it near anything?	How much is the rent?
1. house				
2.			park	
3.	2			
4.				
5.		1		
6.				$1,500

C. **Study the words. Complete the chart with the words.**

kitchen	pool	hall	sofa	bathtub
balcony	porch	driveway	deck	refrigerator

Inside	Outside

D. **Look at the picture and complete the sentences.**

1. The cat is _____ the sofa.

2. The lamp is _____ the sofa.

3. The sofa is _____ the end table and the lamp.

4. The book is _____ the _____.

5. The painting is _____ the sofa.

Review   103

E. Describe the pictures with sentences in the present continuous.

Carmen

Saud

Saud

1. Carmen _____.

2. Saud _____.

3. Saud _____.

F. Write a conversation about finding a home. Make an appointment to see the home.

Owner: _____

You: _____

Owner: _____

You: _____

Owner: _____

You: _____

Owner: _____

You: _____

G. List furniture for each room.

Bedroom	Kitchen	Dining room	Bathroom	Garage	Living room

TEAM PROJECT ✓ Plan a dream home

In this project, you will make a floor plan of a dream home, write a classified ad for the home, and present both to the class.

1. **COLLABORATE** Form a team with four or five students. In your team, you need:

Position	Job description	Student name
Student 1: **Team Leader**	Check that everyone speaks English. Check that everyone participates.	
Student 2: **Architect**	With help from the team, draw the floor plan.	
Student 3: **Decorator**	With help from the team, place furniture in your plan.	
Students 4/5: **Spokespeople**	With help from the team, organize a presentation.	

2. Choose a kind of home. Is it an apartment, house, condominium, or mobile home?

3. Make a floor plan of the home.

4. Make a list of furniture for your home.

5. Decide where to put the furniture.

6. Write a classified ad for your home.

7. Plan a presentation for the class and present your dream home.

EXPLORER BEN HORTON

Photography Protects the World

"Getting people to fall in love with our world is the first step to getting them to protect it."
—Ben Horton

A. PREDICT Answer the questions.

1. Where is Ben Horton?   2. What is he doing?   3. Where does he live?

B. PREDICT Match the information. Draw lines from the question to the answer.

1. What is Ben Horton's job?   a. All over the world.

2. Where does he work?   b. Yosemite National Park.

3. Where is one place he goes?   c. He thinks it is important to protect the planet.

4. What is he interested in?   d. He is a photographer.

C. Read about Ben Horton.

Ben Horton is a photographer. He lives in an apartment in California, but he doesn't stay at his apartment for long. Ben goes on lots of adventures. For example, he often visits Yosemite National Park. He takes pictures to remind people of the beauty in the world. On his adventures he doesn't sleep in a home, but he sleeps in a tent. Does it have a living room? No, it doesn't. Does it have a dining room? No, it doesn't. It's one small, portable room!

D. Answer the questions about Ben Horton's story.

1. In the story, it says Ben Horton *doesn't stay home for long*. What do you think this means?
   a. He is home a lot.
   b. He is not home a lot.
   c. He doesn't like his home.

2. What do you think *adventure* means in the story?
   a. an exciting experience
   b. a portable room
   c. a photographer

3. What do you think *remind* means in the story?
   a. sleeping in a tent
   b. help people remember
   c. beauty

E. CLASSIFY Discuss the words in the box with your teacher and complete the chart.

| bed | dining room | fire | ice chest |
| picnic table | refrigerator | sleeping bag | stove |

Home	Away from home
dining room	

How Your T-Shirt Can Make a Difference

Before You Watch

A. Look at the picture. What do you see? Tell a partner. Then read about cotton.

> Cotton is a plant. It makes cloth. We make clothes and many other things from cotton. It is light and easy to wear. People usually wear cotton when the weather is hot.

B. In groups, look at everyone's clothes. Make a list of the items of clothing.

Women's	Men's

C. Describe your favorite T-shirt. What color is it? What size is it? Is it cotton? How often do you wash it? Use the phrases in the box. Tell a partner.

My favorite T-shirt is (color).	I wash it every week.	My T-shirt is made from cotton.
It is large.	I wash it every day.	It is medium.
It is nice.	It is small.	

D. Read the list. Check each item that you think has cotton in it. Compare your list with a partner.

_____ paper money   _____ bed sheets   _____ living room curtains

_____ towels   _____ a bookbag   _____ a bed

_____ pillows   _____ a sofa   _____ a rug

E. Read the words and their definitions. Then complete the paragraph.

manufacture	to make something with machines
carbon footprint	things you do that affect the environment
transport	to carry or move something from one place to another
loads of washing	amounts of clothes put into a washing machine
buy	use money to pay for something

My family has a clothing business. We (1) _____ cotton T-shirts.

We (2) _____ our T-shirts to stores all over the United States. We

want our business to do well. However, we make choices that don't hurt the environment.

For example, we only (3) _____ from farmers who use less water

to grow cotton. This is important because we want our (4) _____ to

be smaller. We want our customers to do the same. We tell them to do fewer

(5) _____.

While You Watch

F. Watch the video. Read each question. Write an amount.

1. How many T-shirts are in your closet? _____

2. How many T-shirts do you really need? _____

3. How often do you wash and dry your T-shirts? _____

4. How often do you need to wash and dry your T-shirt? _____

G. Watch the video. Then read each sentence. Circle T for *True* or F for *False*.

1. It takes eight cups of water to make one T-shirt.   T   F

2. It takes a lot of energy to grow and care for cotton.   T   F

3. One load of washing uses more energy than one load of drying.   T   F

4. One load of washing uses 40 gallons of water.   T   F

5. It takes more water to make one T-shirt than one person drinks in a day.   T   F

H. Watch the video. Then look at the pie chart. Complete the information with the correct words and numbers.

1	salty	human use
snow	2	97

Earth's Water

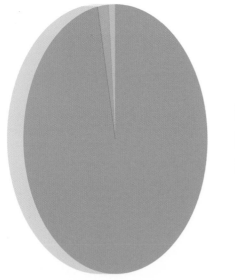

■ 1_____: _____ %

■ 2_____: _____ %

■ 3_____: _____ %

After You Watch

I. **Read each sentence. Choose the answer that is correct for you.**

True = 1 point	*False* = 0 points

Total points _____

1. I buy a new T-shirt every three months.   _____
2. I do a load of washing every day.   _____
3. I use a dryer to dry my clothes.   _____
4. I do not take public transportation.   _____
5. I do not walk or use a bike to go places.   _____
6. I do not turn out the lights when I leave a room.   _____

J. **Compare your answers from Exercise I with a partner. The person with the fewest points has the smaller *carbon footprint*.**

> I think I have a smaller carbon footprint. I only have two points.

> I think I have a larger carbon footprint. I have five points!

K. **Read the question. Then read the list. Check the correct answers.**

How can you make your carbon footprint smaller?

_____ Use cold water to wash clothes

_____ Drive to work and school

_____ Wash three loads of clothing every day

_____ Wear less cotton

_____ Ride a bicycle or walk

_____ Plant a tree

_____ Eat food from your garden

_____ Leave all the lights on in your home

_____ Use more paper

_____ Hang your clothes outside to dry

L. **Complete the columns and the total amount. Discuss the amount of water you use in a day in small groups.**

Activity	Times (per day)	Water (gallons)	Total (gallons)
Washing machine		40 per load	
Bath		35	
Five-minute shower		10	
Brushing teeth		2	
Flushing toilet		3	
Dishwasher		10	

Total number of gallons of water you use per day: _____

UNIT 5
Our Community

Crowds are waiting for the fireworks at Arlington National Cementery.

UNIT OUTCOMES

- [ ] Identify locations and services
- [ ] Give and follow street directions
- [ ] Give and follow directions in a mall
- [ ] Leave a phone message
- [ ] Write an e-mail

Look at the photo and answer the questions.

1. What are the people doing in the picture?
2. Where do you think they are?
3. Are they all facing the same way for a reason?

LESSON ① Places and services

GOAL ▪ Identify locations and services

A. INTERPRET Look at the web page with your classmates and teacher. Talk about the different sections.

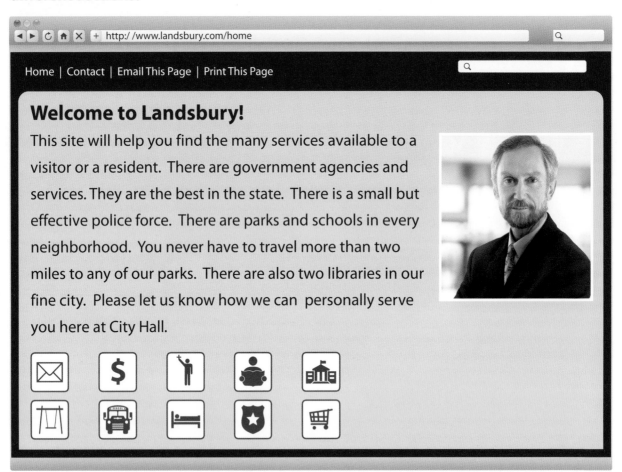

B. INFER Make a list of government agencies and services in Landsbury based on the reading.

ONE OR MORE

There **is** a police station.

There **are** parks and schools.

1. public libraries

2. _____

3. _____

4. _____

5. _____

C. **CLASSIFY** Work in a group. Write the words from the box under the correct pictures below.

apartment	hostel	hotel	dentist's office
tennis court	hospital	motel	doctor's office
mobile home	playground	house	park

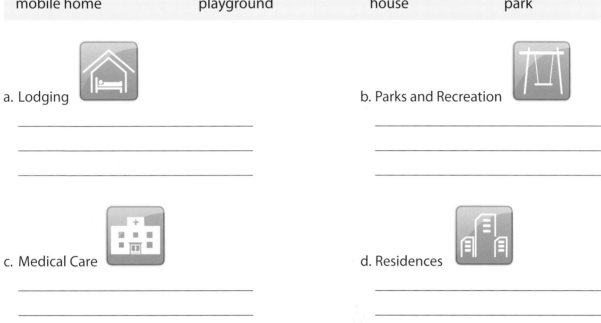

a. Lodging

_____

_____

_____

b. Parks and Recreation

_____

_____

_____

c. Medical Care

_____

_____

_____

d. Residences

_____

_____

_____

D. Listen. Write the number under the correct picture.

CD 2
TR 1

_____

_____

_____

_____

_____

_____

Lesson 1 115

E.   PREDICT   Look at the picture. What are they doing? Who are they calling?

Fire 911
Police 911
Jefferson Memorial Bank 555-3232
Landsbury Hospital 555-7665
Post Office 555-8444
DMV 555-3722

F.   Listen to the conversation. Practice the conversation with new information.

CD 2
TR 2

Emanuela: I need to call the <u>hospital</u>.
Lisa: Why?
Emanuela: <u>My sister is very sick.</u>
Lisa: The number is <u>555-7665</u>.

Place	Problem	Phone number
hospital	My sister is very sick.	555-7665
bank	I need to get some money from my account.	555-4856
DMV	I need a driver's license.	555-7698
post office	I need to send a letter.	555-2047

G.   SURVEY   Make a bar graph for your class. How many students go to these places?

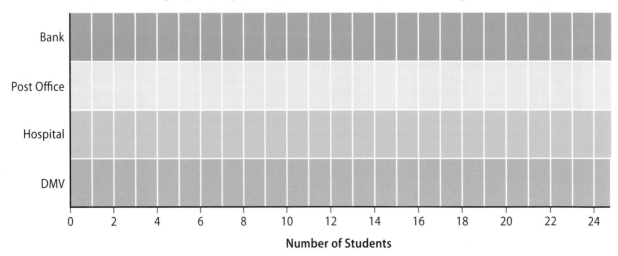

Number of Students

H.   APPLY   Find a telephone directory or look on the Internet. Make a list of important numbers to put on your phone at home.

LESSON 2 Where is City Hall?

GOAL ▪ Give and follow street directions

A. Discuss the phrases with your teacher.

turn left

go straight ahead

It's on the left.

turn right

turn around

It's on the right.

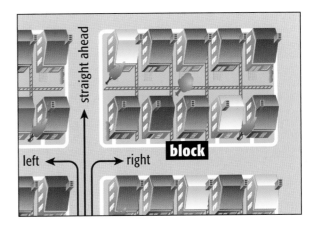

B. Look at the picture. Where is Gabriela? What is she doing? Then, practice the conversation.

Alma: I need to find City Hall.

Gabriela: Of course. Go straight ahead one block and turn right.

Alma: Can you repeat that slowly for me?

Gabriela: Sure. That's straight ahead one block... Turn right... It's on the left.

Alma: Thanks.

Gabriela: No problem.

C. Make new conversations. Use the information below. Use Exercise B as a model.

Place	Directions
1. bus station	Go straight ahead one block and turn right. Go one block and turn right. Go one block. It's on the left.
2. City Hall	Go straight ahead one block and turn right. It's on the left.
3. Rosco's Buffet Restaurant	Go straight ahead two blocks and turn left. It's on the right.
4. post office	Go straight ahead one block and turn right. Go one more block and turn left. It's on the right.
5. zoo	Go straight ahead two blocks and turn right. It's on the right.
6. high school	Go straight ahead two blocks and turn right. Go one more block and turn right. It's on the left.

D. Look at the map. Read the directions from Exercise C on page 117. Number the places 1–6 in the squares on the map.

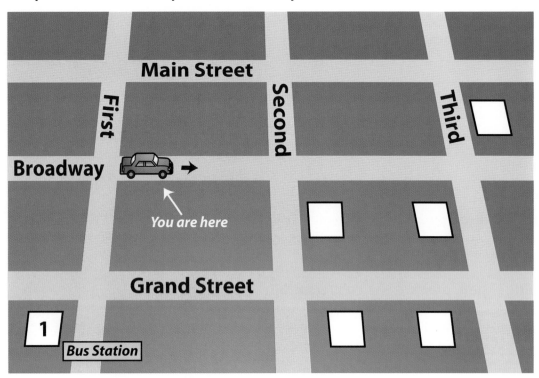

E. **ANALYZE** Where are the places? Look at the map and complete the table.

Place	Location
1. bus station	The bus station is on Grand Street.
2. City Hall	
3. Rosco's Buffet Restaurant	
4. post office	
5. zoo	
6. high school	

F. Practice the conversation with information from Exercise E.

Student A: Where is the bus station?
Student B: It's on Grand Street in Landsbury.

IN / ON

in the city

on the street

It's *on* Main Street *in* Landsbury.

G. Write the phrases under the signs.

| Turn right | Turn left | Turn around | Go straight |

_____   _____   _____   _____

H. Listen and check (✓) the boxes for the phrases you hear.

CD 2
TR 3-7

	Turn right	Turn left	Turn around	Go straight
1. Directions to the mall	✓		✓	✓
2. Directions to the post office				
3. Directions to the movie theater				
4. Directions to the museum				
5. Directions to the park				

I. Ask four classmates and complete the chart.

Student A: Where do you live, Herman?
Student B: I live <u>in</u> Landsbury <u>on</u> Maple Avenue.

Student name	City	Street
1. Herman	Landsbury	Maple Avenue
2.		
3.		
4.		
5.		

L E S S O N ③ Let's go to the mall!

GOAL ▪ Give and follow directions in a mall

A. INTERPRET Answer the questions about the directory.

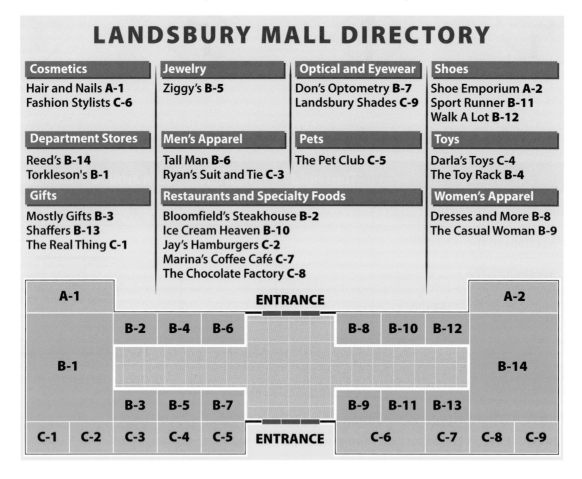

LANDSBURY MALL DIRECTORY

Cosmetics
Hair and Nails **A-1**
Fashion Stylists **C-6**

Jewelry
Ziggy's **B-5**

Optical and Eyewear
Don's Optometry **B-7**
Landsbury Shades **C-9**

Shoes
Shoe Emporium **A-2**
Sport Runner **B-11**
Walk A Lot **B-12**

Department Stores
Reed's **B-14**
Torkleson's **B-1**

Men's Apparel
Tall Man **B-6**
Ryan's Suit and Tie **C-3**

Pets
The Pet Club **C-5**

Toys
Darla's Toys **C-4**
The Toy Rack **B-4**

Gifts
Mostly Gifts **B-3**
Shaffers **B-13**
The Real Thing **C-1**

Restaurants and Specialty Foods
Bloomfield's Steakhouse **B-2**
Ice Cream Heaven **B-10**
Jay's Hamburgers **C-2**
Marina's Coffee Café **C-7**
The Chocolate Factory **C-8**

Women's Apparel
Dresses and More **B-8**
The Casual Woman **B-9**

1. What store is next to Tall Man? _____

2. What store is next to Dresses and More? _____

3. What store is between The Pet Club and Ryan's Suit and Tie? _____

4. What store is between Landsbury Shades and Marina's Coffee Cafe? _____

B. SCAN Scan the directory. Take turns asking and answering the questions with a partner.

1. Where can you buy a dog?

2. Where can you buy a suit for a man?

3. Where can you buy ice cream?

4. Where can you buy sneakers?

5. Where can you eat a steak?

120 Unit 5

C. **Study the information with your teacher. Listen for the prepositions.**

around the corner	next to	on the corner	between	across from

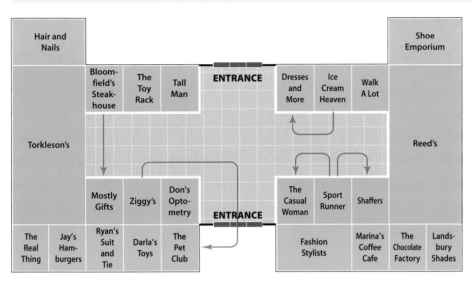

D. **Listen again and complete the sentences.**

1. The Casual Woman is _____ Sport Runner.

2. Jay's Hamburgers is _____ the corner.

3. Jay's Hamburgers is _____ the Real Thing and Ryan's Suit and Tie.

E. **Write sentences about the mall diagram in Exercise C.**

1. Jay's Hamburgers / Ryan's Suit and Tie
   Jay's Hamburgers is next to Ryan's Suit and Tie.
   _____

2. Ziggy's / The Pet Club
   _____

3. The Casual Woman / Dresses and More
   _____

4. Landsbury Shades
   _____

5. Sport Runner / Shaffers / The Casual Woman
   _____

6. Fashion Stylists / Marina's Coffee Café
   _____

F. Student A looks at page 121 and Student B looks at page 122. Student B asks where Ice Cream Heaven, Shoe Emporium, and the Pet Club are. Write the information on the diagram.

Student B: Where's Ice Cream Heaven?

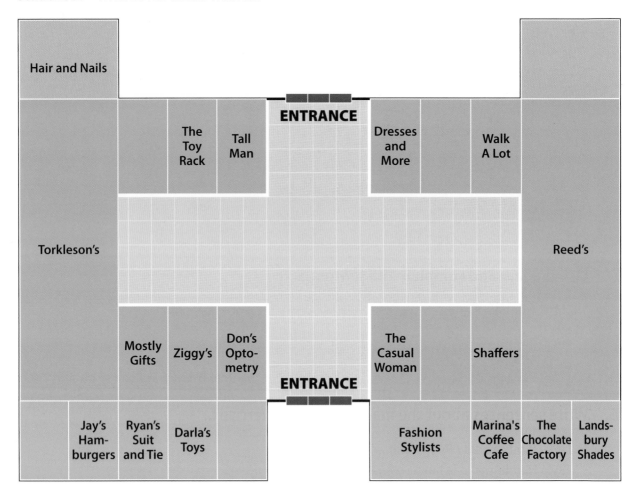

G. Student B looks at page 121 and Student A looks at page 122. Student A asks where Sport Runner, The Real Thing, and Bloomfield's Steakhouse are. Write the information on the diagram.

Student A: Where is Sport Runner?

H. **DESIGN** In groups, create a mall directory and floor plan. Then, share with the class.

GOAL ▢ Leave a phone message

A. INTERPRET Look at the package. Who is the package from? Who is the package to? Then, read about Gabriela's problem.

From | Gabriela Ramirez
37 Main Street
Landsbury, WA
99037

CLEARED

9781304568791

TO | Familia Ramirez
Av. Callao 423
1022 Buenos Aires,
Argentina

FRAGILE

Gabriela has a problem. She needs to go to the post office. She wants to send a package to her family in Buenos Aires, Argentina. She doesn't know what to say at the post office.

B. EVALUATE What can Gabriela do? Who can help her? Talk in a group and complete the sentences below.

1. She can ask _____.

2. She can call _____.

3. She can go _____.

C. Listen to Gabriela leave a message. Circle the answers.

CD 2
TR 9

1. Who does she talk to?
   a. her friend David
   b. a machine
   c. David, her brother

2. When does she want to go to the post office?
   a. today
   b. tomorrow
   c. Saturday

D. There are three important parts of a message. Read the chart with your classmates and teacher.

Your name	Reason for calling	Your phone number
Gabriela	I have a question.	My number is 555-2344.
	I want to talk.	Call me at 555-2344.
	I need some information.	Can you call me back at 555-2344?

E. **EVALUATE** Look at the messages. Talk in a group. Circle the good messages.

1. This is Gabriela. I need help. I want to send a package. Please call me at 555-2344. Thanks.

2. Call me. OK?

3. I am Gabriela. My phone number is 555-2344.

4. This is your friend Gabriela from school. My number is 555-2344. Please call me. I have a question for you. Thanks.

5. This is Gabriela. My number is 555-2344. I have a small problem. Can you call me back? Thanks.

F. Practice leaving a message with two classmates.

Student A: Hello, this is Gabriela. I can't come to the phone right now. Please leave a message.

Student B: This is Ramon. I have a question. My number is 555-2125.

Name: _____

Phone number: _____

Reason for calling: _____

_____

_____

Name: _____

Phone number: _____

Reason for calling: _____

_____

_____

G. **Study the chart with your classmates and teacher.**

Questions with *Can*			
Can	**Subject**	**Base verb**	**Example question**
Can	I you	help ask talk answer call	**Can** I help you? **Can** I ask you a question? **Can** I talk to you? **Can** you answer a question? **Can** you call me?

H. **Match the questions with the responses. There may be more than one correct response.**

1. Can you help me?

2. Can I ask you a question?

3. Can I talk to you?

4. Can you answer a question?

5. Can you call me?

a. Yes. What's the question?

b. I can call you tomorrow.

c. Sure. What can I do for you?

d. OK. What can we talk about?

e. Yes. What's the question?

I. **Write questions. Put the words in the correct order.**

1. help / can / I / you
   Can I help you?

2. answer / the question / I / can

3. I / talk / to you / can / tomorrow

4. I / can / you / see / tomorrow

J. **APPLY** **Write a message you can leave for a friend on an answering machine for each situation.**

I am very sick. _____

I have a problem. _____

I don't understand. _____

LESSON **5** Dear Mom

GOAL ▢ Write an e-mail

A. INTERPRET Read Gabriela's e-mail to her family.

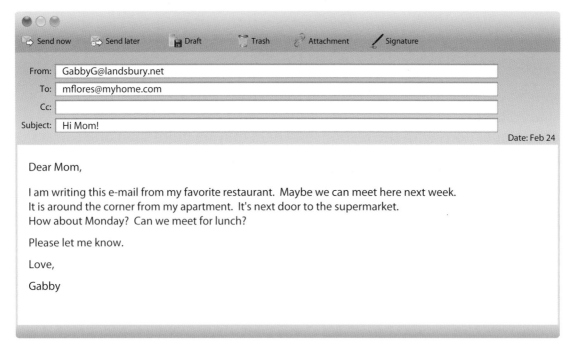

B. Answer the questions about the e-mail.

1. What is Gabriela's e-mail address?

   _____

2. What is her mother's e-mail address?

   _____

3. Where is the supermarket?

   _____

4. When did she write the e-mail?

   _____

5. Who is the e-mail to?

   _____

6. Where is Gabriela writing the e-mail from?

   _____

C. Study the charts with your classmates and teacher.

Present Continuous				
Subject	*Be*	**Base** + *ing*	**Time**	**Example sentence**
I	am (I'm)	writing		I'**m writing** a letter right now.
He, She, It	is (she's)	eating	right now today	She'**s eating** a sandwich.
You, We, They	are (they're)	reading		They'**re reading** a book today.

D. Complete the sentences with the present continuous form of the verb in parentheses.

1. She _____is eating_____ (eat) at a restaurant.

2. They _____ (write) e-mail.

3. We _____ (read) e-mail.

SPELLING
write → writing

4. I _____ (go) to the hospital. I am very sick.

5. Gabriela _____ (buy) a book at the bookstore right now.

Simple Present			
Subject	**Adverb**	**Verb**	**Example sentence**
I	always often	write	I always **write** e-mails.
He, She, It	sometimes	eats	He rarely **eats** here.
You, We, They	rarely never	read	They never **read** the newspaper.

Adverbs of Frequency

0%   50%   100%

never   rarely   sometimes   usually   always

E. Complete the sentences with the simple present form of the verb in parentheses.

1. She _____lives_____ (live) in Landsbury.

2. I never _____ (read) classified ads.

3. We rarely _____ (study) on Saturday.

4. They often _____ (write) e-mails or texts at lunchtime.

5. You _____ (go) to school at the Orangewood School for Adults.

SPELLING
study → stud**ies**

F. Listen and answer the questions.

CD 2
TR 10

1. Where do you go to school? _I go to_____.

2. Where do you live? _I live_____.

3. Where is a restaurant nearby? _A restaurant is_____.

4. What do you sometimes do? _I sometimes_____.

G. Ask a partner questions and write his or her answers.

1. Where do you go to school?

_He (She) goes to_____._

2. Where do you live?

_____

3. Where is a restaurant nearby?

_____

4. What do you sometimes do?

_____

H. COMPOSE Write the text for an e-mail to a family member about your city. Use the information about yourself and your partner from this page.

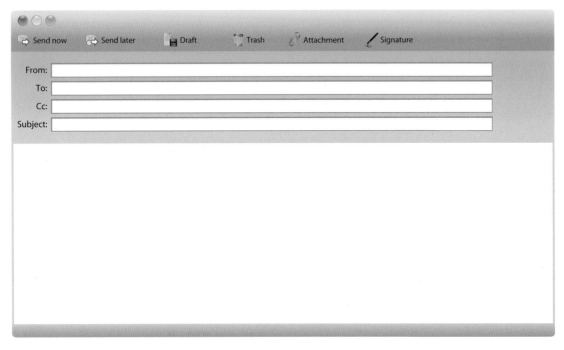

I. APPLY Write a real e-mail to friends or family. Get an e-mail account if necessary.

Before You Watch

A. Look at the picture. Complete each sentence.

1. Naomi, Hector, and Mateo are

   in a _____.

2. Hector and Mateo are

   _____.

3. Mateo is _____.

While You Watch

B. ▶ **Watch the video. How do you get from the bookstore to the diner? Write numbers to show the correct order.**

a. _____ Then turn right.

b. _____ Go toward City Hall.

c. _____ The diner is on the left.

d. _____ Walk one block.

e. __1__ Walk down Atlantic for two blocks.

Check Your Understanding

C. Complete the dialog. Use the words in the box.

on the corner of	~~in front of~~	on	signs	straight

Mateo: I'm (1) ___in front of___ the bookstore. The bookstore is next to a coffee shop.

Naomi: Ask him what street he's (2) _____.

Hector: What street are you on? Do you see any street (3) _____?

Mateo: Yeah, I'm (4) _____ Atlantic and Broadway.

Hector: He's on the corner of Atlantic and Broadway.

Naomi: Tell him to walk (5) _____ for two blocks.

Review

Learner Log

I can list places and services.
■ Yes ■ No ■ Maybe

I can give and follow street directions.
■ Yes ■ No ■ Maybe

A. Look at the map. Ask a partner for the location of each place.

the motel	the mobile homes	the hospital
the park	the apartments	the hotel
the public pool	the post office	

Student A: Where are the tennis courts?

Student B: They are on Second Street, next to the post office.

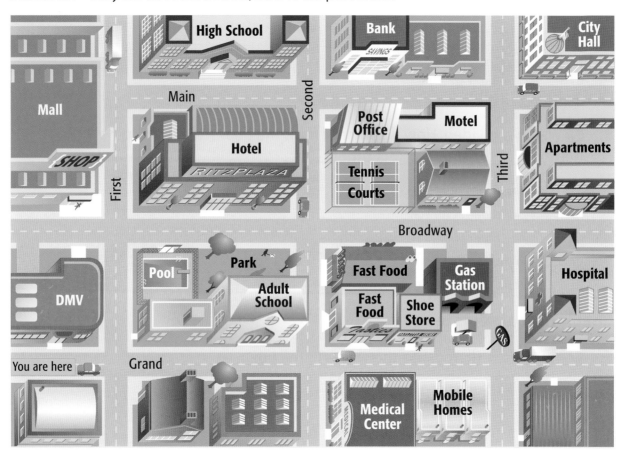

B. Give directions to a partner to each location.

the hotel	the apartments	City Hall
the hospital	the high school	the bank
the motel	the DMV	

Student A: Can you give me directions to the medical center?

Student B: Yes, go straight ahead on Grand. Go one block. It's on the right.

Learner Log

I can give and follow directions in a mall.   I can leave a phone message.
☐ Yes ☐ No ☐ Maybe   ☐ Yes ☐ No ☐ Maybe

CD 2
TR 11

C. **Listen to the messages. Complete the chart.**

Name	Reason for calling	Phone number
1. Nadia	I have a question.	555-2134
2. Vien		
3. David		
4. Ricardo		

D. **Write sentences about yourself.**

I always _____.

I often _____.

Sometimes I _____.

I rarely _____.

I never _____.

E. **With a group, list the types of stores you can find at a mall.**

_____   _____

_____   _____

_____   _____

_____   _____

_____   _____

_____   _____

F. **Read the services in the box. Then, write them under the correct places below.**

| a. Delivers mail | b. Helps sick people | c. Keeps your money safe | d. Gives licenses |

1.

_____

2.

_____

3.

_____

4.

_____

G. **Write a new e-mail. Use the model on page 126.**

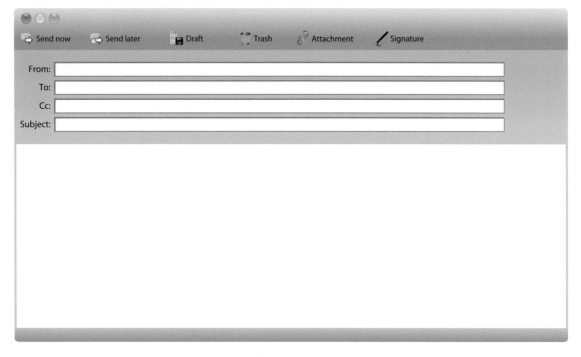

Make a brochure of a new city

In this project, you will make a brochure of a new city and present it to the class.

1. **COLLABORATE** Form a team with four or five students. In your team, you need:

Position	Job description	Student name
Student 1: **Team Leader**	Check that everyone speaks English. Check that everyone participates.	
Student 2: **City Planner**	With help from the team, draw a map of your city.	
Student 3: **Artist**	With help from the team, make a brochure of your city.	
Students 4/5: **Spokespeople**	With help from the team, organize a presentation to give to the class.	

2. Choose a name for your city.

3. Make a list of important places in your city and put them in alphabetical order.

4. Make a map of your city and mark where the important places are.

5. Make a brochure. On the brochure, write one paragraph about the city, write the names of your team's members, and draw a picture that represents the city.

6. Prepare a presentation for the class.

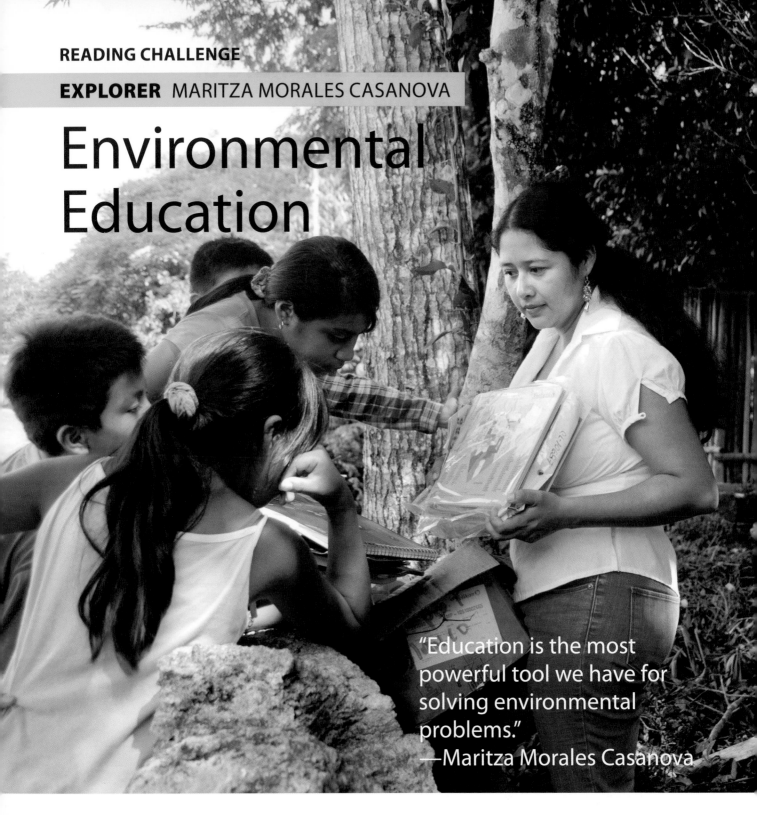

EXPLORER MARITZA MORALES CASANOVA

Environmental Education

"Education is the most powerful tool we have for solving environmental problems."
—Maritza Morales Casanova

A. PREDICT Before you read about Maritza, look at the title and photo above. Answer the questions.

1. What does *environment* mean?

   a. the natural world around us

   b. people in a country

   c. children

2. What are the children in the picture doing?

   a. They are eating lunch.

   b. They are learning about the environment.

   c. They are hiking.

B. Look at the blueprints of an environmental park in Yucatan, Mexico. Describe to a partner where things are located.

Student 1: Where are <u>the offices</u>?
Student 2: They are <u>on the right</u>.

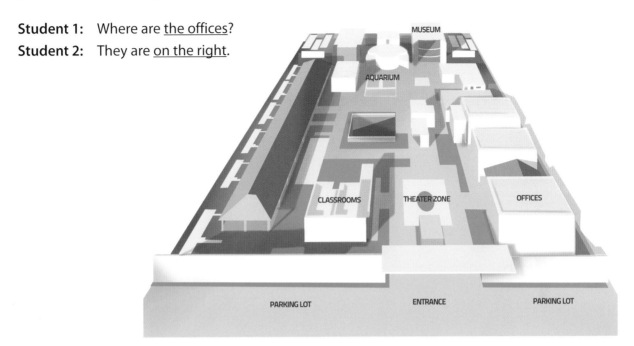

C. Read about Maritza Morales Casanova and her community.

Maritza Morales Casanova is <u>working</u> hard to teach children about the environment. On July 24th, 2013, she opened an environmental park in Yucatan, Mexico, called Ceiba Pentandra Park. The park is a little community. The plan for the park shows the different areas. The classrooms are <u>on the left</u>. The offices are <u>on the right</u>. The Theatre Zone is <u>between</u> the classrooms and the offices. At the school, children are the teachers. They teach other children how to take care of the planet.

D. Answer the questions about the paragraph.

1. **What** is the name of the park? _____

2. **Where** is the park? _____

3. **When** did the park open? _____

4. **Who** are the teachers? _____

E. **RANK** In a group, rank ways to save the environment. 1 is for the best way.

_____ Walk or ride a bike instead of driving.   _____ Don't use the heater too much.

_____ Use recycled paper.   _____ Take showers, not baths.

_____ Don't use the air conditioner too much.   _____ Take short showers.

Health and Fitness

New York City residents run in a marathon across the Verrazano-Narrows Bridge.

UNIT OUTCOMES

- Identify parts of the body
- Identify illnesses and health problems
- Give advice
- Ask for information
- Develop an exercise plan

Look at the photo and answer the questions.

1. Where are the people?
2. What are they doing?
3. Do you think they are healthy? Why?

GOAL ▪ Identify parts of the body

A. PREDICT Look at the picture. Who is Victor talking to? What is the problem? Then, read about Victor.

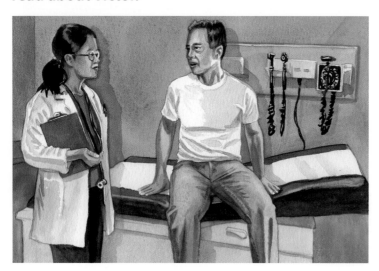

Victor is sick. He visits the doctor. The doctor asks, "What is the problem?" Victor answers, "I hurt all over. I think I have a fever. My head hurts and my muscles ache." The doctor checks Victor for the flu. The doctor gives him some medicine for the pain.

B. Circle *True* or *False*.

1. Victor needs medicine.	True	False
2. Victor's head hurts.	True	False
3. Victor doesn't have a problem.	True	False

C. INFER Victor says, "I hurt all over." Make a list of body parts that you think he means:

_____head_____

_____

_____

_____

_____

_____

D. Label the parts of the body. Use the words from the boxes.

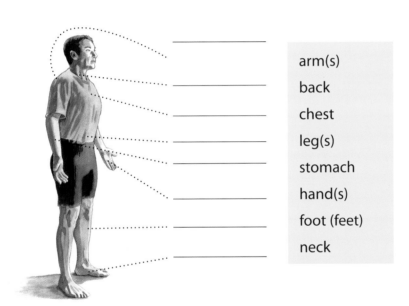

nose

mouth

head

tooth (teeth)

ear(s)

eye(s)

_____

_____

_____

_____

_____

_____

_____

_____

_____

_____

_____

_____

_____

arm(s)

back

chest

leg(s)

stomach

hand(s)

foot (feet)

neck

CD 2
TR 12-14

E. Listen to the patients talk to the doctor. What are their problems? Complete the sentences.

1. **Karen:** Doctor, my _____ hurts.

2. **Roberto:** Doctor, my _____ hurts.

3. **Tino:** Doctor, my _____ and _____ hurt.

F. Read the conversation. Practice new conversations using the words in Exercise D.

Doctor: What is the problem today?

Patient: My <u>leg hurts.</u>

Doctor: Your <u>leg</u>?

Patient: Yes, my <u>leg</u>.

G. Study the chart with your classmates and teacher.

Simple Present		
Subject	**Verb**	**Example sentence**
It My leg My arm My foot My head	hurts	My leg **hurts.** My arm **hurts.** My head **hurts.**
They My legs My arms My feet My ears	hurt	My legs **hurt.** My feet **hurt.** My ears **hurt.**

H. Write sentences for singular and plural subjects.

Part of body	Singular	Plural
leg	My leg hurts.	My legs hurt.
arm	My arm hurts.	My arms hurt.
head		
foot		
back		
eye		
nose		
ear		

I. **APPLY** In a group, create a list of body parts from the lesson. Discuss what hurts more often.

LESSON **2** What's the problem?

GOAL ◼ Identify illnesses and health problems

A. Label the picture with the words from the box.

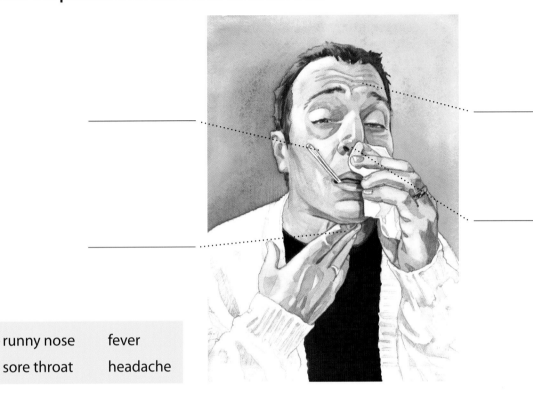

runny nose	fever
sore throat	headache

B. Listen and practice the conversation.

CD 2
TR 15

Doctor:	What's the matter?
Miguel:	Doctor, I feel very sick. I have a terrible sore throat.
Doctor:	You have the flu.
Miguel:	The flu?
Doctor:	Yes, the flu!

> **INTONATION**
>
> **Intonation: Information Questions**
>
> What's the matter?
>
> **Intonation: Clarification Questions**
>
> The flu?

C. Listen to each conversation. Circle the problem.

CD 2
TR 16-19

1. sore throat	runny nose	fever	headache
2. sore throat	runny nose	fever	headache
3. sore throat	runny nose	fever	headache
4. sore throat	runny nose	fever	headache

D. ANALYZE Read about colds and the flu. Then, complete the chart.

> Every year people have both colds and the flu. What is the difference? Usually a person with a cold or the flu has a headache and a sore throat. A person with a cold sometimes has a low fever, and a person with the flu has a high fever and muscle aches. Cold symptoms also include a runny nose. Flu symptoms include a dry cough.

Common cold symptoms	Common flu symptoms
	high fever
sore throat	
	headache
runny nose	
	dry cough

E. COMPARE Complete the diagram using the information in Exercise D.

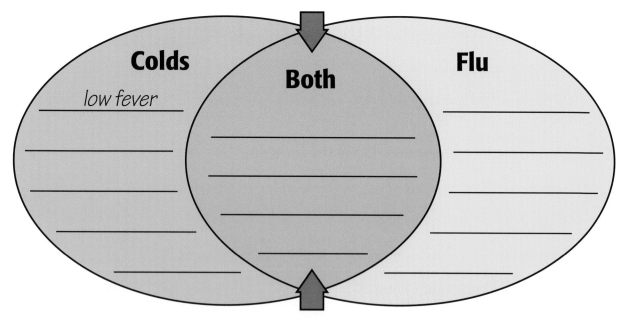

F. Study the charts with your classmates and teacher.

Simple Present: *Have*		
Subject	*Have*	**Example sentence**
I, You, We, They	have	I **have** a headache. You **have** a sore throat.
He, She, It	has	She **has** a stomachache. He **has** a fever.

Negative Simple Present: *Have*			
Subject	**Negative**	*Have*	**Example sentence**
I, You, We, They	do not (don't)	have	I **don't have** a headache. You **don't have** a sore throat.
He, She, It	does not (doesn't)	have	She **doesn't have** a stomachache. He **doesn't have** a fever.

G. Complete the sentences with the correct form of the verb.

Armando

headache,
stomachache, fever

Yusuf

headache,
sore throat, cough

Lien

sore throat,
stomachache, backache

1. Armando _____ a headache.

2. Armando and Yusuf _____ backaches.

3. Yusuf _____ a cough.

4. Lien _____ a fever.

5. Armando and Lien _____ stomachaches.

6. Yusuf and Lien _____ sore throats.

H. What other illnesses do you know? Use a dictionary and list illnesses and symptoms in your notebook.

LESSON ③ What should I do?

GOAL ■ Give advice

A. Look at the pictures. Study the words and phrases with your classmates and teacher.

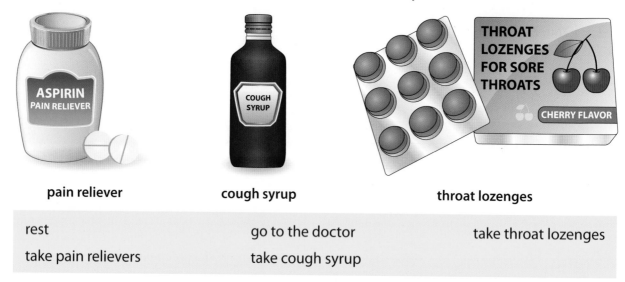

pain reliever   cough syrup   throat lozenges

| rest | go to the doctor | take throat lozenges |
| take pain relievers | take cough syrup | |

B. **EVALUATE** What do you do when you have these symptoms? Complete the chart.

Symptom	Take pain relievers	Rest	Take cough syrup	Take throat lozenges	Go to the doctor	Other
fever						
cough						
headache	✓					✓
sore throat						
stomachache						
backache						
feel tired						

C. Practice the conversation. Then, use information from Exercise B to make new conversations.

Patient: I have <u>a headache</u>.
Doctor: <u>Take pain relievers</u>.
Patient: Thanks.

144 Unit 6

D. PREDICT Look at the picture. What is Karen talking about? What is the doctor writing? Then, read about Karen.

Karen is talking to the doctor. Karen is sick. She has a bad headache and sore throat. The doctor is giving Karen a prescription for some medicine. She needs to read the labels on the medicine carefully. The doctor is helping her understand them.

E. Read the statements. Circle *True* or *False*.

1. Karen is sick. She has a backache.   True   False

2. The doctor doesn't give Karen medicine.   True   False

3. Karen should read the labels.   True   False

F. Read the labels.

INSTRUCTIONS
Take two tablets every three hours.

Take two tablespoons every four hours.

Instructions
Take one lozenge as needed for sore throat pain.

CHERRY FLAVOR

G. Listen to Karen reading the medicine labels. Write the medicine for each description.

CD 2
TR 20

1. _____   2. _____   3. _____

H. Study the charts with your classmates and teacher.

Should for Advice			
Subject	*should*	**Base verb**	**Example sentence**
I, You, He, She, It, We, They	should	rest	You **should** rest.
		stay	He **should** stay home.
		go	They **should** see a doctor.
		take	I **should** take pain relievers.
			We **should** take cough syrup.

Should (Negative) for Advice			
Subject	*should*	**Base verb**	**Example sentence**
I, You, He, She, It, We, They	should not (shouldn't)	drive	You **shouldn't** drive and take this medicine.
		drink	He **shouldn't** drink alcohol with this medicine.
		go	We **shouldn't** go out.

I. Read each problem and give advice. Use *should* and *shouldn't*.

1. Roberto has a cold.

   He should take cold medicine, and he shouldn't go out.

2. Anh and Nam have a cold.

   They _____.

3. Michael has a sore throat.

   He _____.

4. Ayumi has a fever.

   She _____.

5. Oscar feels tired.

   He _____.

6. Omar has a stomachache.

   He _____.

J. APPLY In a group, make a list of medications you have in your home and what they are good for.

LESSON **4** There's an emergency!

GOAL ■ Ask for information

A. PREDICT Look at the picture. What is the problem? What is Victor doing? Then, listen and practice the conversation.

CD 2
TR 21

Operator:	What is the emergency?
Victor:	There is a car accident.
Operator:	Where is the accident?
Victor:	It's on Fourth and Bush.
Operator:	What is your name?
Victor:	It's Victor Karaskov.
Operator:	Is anyone hurt?
Victor:	Yes. Please send an ambulance.

B. Answer the questions.

1. Who is calling about the emergency? _____

2. What is the emergency? _____

3. Where is the emergency? _____

C. INTERPRET With a partner, make a new conversation. Use one of the ideas in the chart below.

Who	What	Where
Antonio	A man is having a heart attack.	Broadway and Nutwood
Karen	There is a car accident.	First and Grand
Tran	A house is on fire.	234 Jones Avenue

D. INTERPRET Write the letters next to the correct symbols.

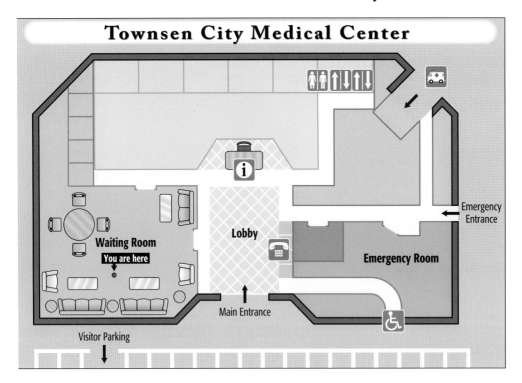

a. the wheelchair entrance   b. the restrooms   c. the elevators

d. Information   e. the pay phones   f. the ambulance entrance

1. _____

2. _____

3. _____

4. _____

5. _____

6. _____

> **IS / ARE**
>
> Where **is** Information?
>
> **It is** here.
>
> Where **are** the restrooms?
>
> **They are** here.

E. Practice the conversations. Ask questions about places in the directory.

Student A: Excuse me, where is Information?
Student B: It's here. (Student B points to the map.)

Student B: Excuse me, where are the elevators?
Student A: They are here. (Student A points to the map.)

Listen to the conversations. Complete the sentences.

1. The elevators are close to the _____.

2. The wheelchair entrance is in the _____.

3. The pay phones are close to the _____.

4. Information is in the _____.

G. **Ask a partner for information. Ask about the elevators, the wheelchair entrance, the pay phones, and Information.**

Student A: Where are the restrooms?
Student B: They are close to the elevators.

H. **CREATE** **In groups of four, prepare a role-play.**

Student 1: You work at the Information desk.
Student 2: You are very sick.
Student 3: You are a family member.
Student 4: You are a nurse.

I. **Find a hospital directory on the Internet. Share the information you find with the class.**

GOAL ■ Develop an exercise plan

A. **Look at the picture. Why is exercise important? Then, read about exercise.**

> We need to exercise. It is good for our heart, muscles, flexibility, and weight. Everyone should exercise. People can run, swim, clean the house, or work in the yard. Doctors say we should exercise every day.

B. **Write the letters of the pictures next to the words.**

_____ 1. muscles   _____ 2. weight   _____ 3. flexibility   _____ 4. heart

a.    b.    c.    d.

C. **ANALYZE** Study the bar graph and answer the questions about Alta, Wisconsin.

Alta, Wisconsin (Exercise Per Week)

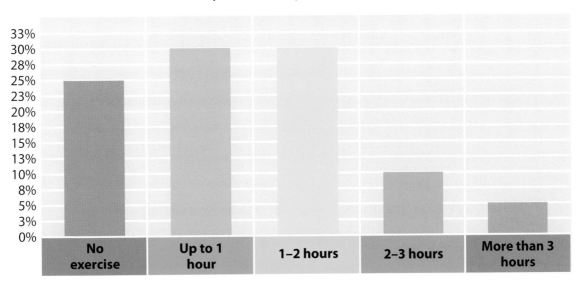

1. What percentage of people don't exercise?

   a. 0%   b. 30%   c. 10%   d. 25%

2. What percentage of people exercise more than three hours a week?

   a. 5%   b. 30%   c. 10%   d. 25%

3. What percentage of people exercise more than one hour a week?

   a. 0%   b. 30%   c. 45%   d. 50%

🎧 **D.** **Listen to the conversations about exercise. Write the number under the correct picture.**

CD 2
TR 26-29

a.

_____

b.

_____

c.

_____

d.

_____

E. **Study the chart with your classmates and teacher.**

Infinitives			
Subject	**Verb**	**Infinitive (*to* + base)**	**Example sentence**
I, You, We, They	want	to run to exercise to walk	I want **to run.** We want **to exercise.** They want **to walk.**
He, She, It	wants	to ride to do to go	He wants **to ride** a bicycle. She wants **to do** yard work. She wants **to go** to the gym.

F. **APPLY** **Write three exercise goals. Use the ideas in Exercise D.**

1. _I want to_____._

2. _____._

3. _____._

G. **Ask three classmates about their exercise goals. Write their goals.**

1. _She/He wants to_____._

2. _____._

3. _____._

H. **SURVEY** **Talk to four classmates. Complete the chart.**

Student A: How much do you exercise every week?

Student B: I exercise about one hour every week.

Amount of Exercise per Week					
Name	**0 minutes**	**0–1 hour**	**1–2 hours**	**2–3 hours**	**more than 3 hours**

You'd better call the doctor

Before You Watch

A. Look at the picture. Complete each sentence.

1. Mr. Sanchez has a

   back_____.

2. He has a _____ in his mouth.

3. Hector is going to

   _____.

While You Watch

B. ▶ Watch the video. Check Mr. Sanchez's symptoms.

Symptom		Symptom	
headache	✔	sore throat	
dizziness		backache	
fever		shoulder ache	
stomachache		runny nose	

Check Your Understanding

C. Match the statements and responses.

Patient

1. My back aches.

2. I have a sore throat.

3. I'm tired all the time.

4. I have a bad headache.

5. I cut my finger.

Doctor

a. Have some aspirin.

b. Take a pain reliever.

c. You need to get more rest.

d. I will clean it with alcohol.

e. You should take some throat lozenges.

Review

Learner Log

I can identify body parts.
☐ Yes ☐ No ☐ Maybe

I can identify symptoms.
☐ Yes ☐ No ☐ Maybe

A. Look at the picture. Write the words.

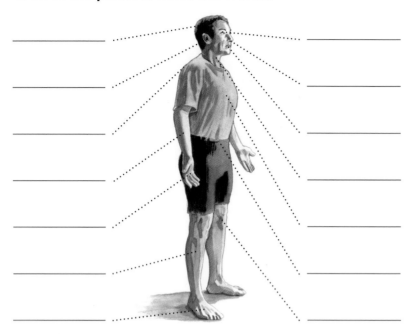

_____

_____

_____

_____

_____

_____

_____

_____

_____

_____

_____

_____

B. Look at the pictures and complete the sentences.

1. My _____ hurt.

2. I have a _____.

3. I have a _____.

4. I have an _____.

5. My _____ hurts.

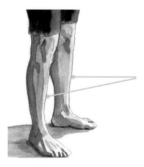

6. My _____ hurt.

C. Match the symptom and the remedy.

_____ 1. fever

_____ 2. feel tired

_____ 3. sore throat

_____ 4. cough

a. lozenges

b. syrup

c. rest

d. pain reliever

D. Practice the conversation with a partner. Make similar conversations.

Student A: What's the matter?

Student B: I have a headache.

Student A: You should take a pain reliever.

Student B: Thanks. That's a good idea.

E. Read the medicine bottles and complete the chart.

1.

Indications:
For minor sore throat pain.

Directions:
Take two tablespoons every four hours.

Warning:
Not for children under 12 years of age.

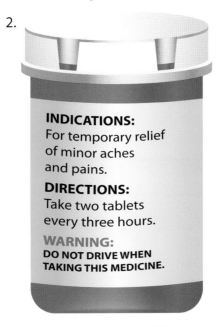

2.

INDICATIONS:
For temporary relief of minor aches and pains.

DIRECTIONS:
Take two tablets every three hours.

WARNING:
DO NOT DRIVE WHEN TAKING THIS MEDICINE.

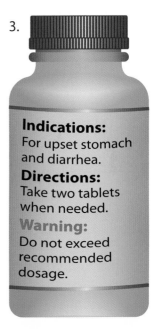

3.

Indications:
For upset stomach and diarrhea.

Directions:
Take two tablets when needed.

Warning:
Do not exceed recommended dosage.

	How many?	How often?
1.	two tablespoons	every four hours
2.		
3.		

F. **Complete the sentences with *should* or *shouldn't*.**

should

1. He ___should___ take medicine.

2. We _____ rest.

3. They _____ go to the doctor.

4. We _____ exercise every day.

shouldn't

1. I _____ drink and drive.

2. He _____ take four tablets.

3. We _____ go out.

4. They _____ drive and take this medicine.

G. **Read the conversation and put the sentences in the correct order.**

_____ **Victor:**   There's a car accident.

___1___ **Operator:**   911, what is the emergency?

_____ **Victor:**   Yes.

_____ **Victor:**   It's on Fourth and Bush.

_____ **Operator:**   Is anyone hurt?

_____ **Operator:**   OK. The police and ambulance are on the way.

_____ **Operator:**   Where is the accident?

H. **Write six items you can find in a hospital.**

_____   _____   _____

_____   _____   _____

I. **Ask three classmates about their exercise goals. Complete the chart.**

Name	What exercise do you want to do?	When do you want to do this exercise?	How long do you want to do this exercise?
Nadia	swim	8 a.m. on Saturdays	40 minutes

TEAM PROJECT ✓ **Create a role-play about an emergency**

In this project, you will create a role-play. Members of your group will be a patient, a family member, a 911 operator, a doctor, and a hospital worker.

1. **COLLABORATE** Form a team with four or five students. In your team, you need:

Position	Job description	Student name
Student 1: **Team Leader**	Check that everyone speaks English. Check that everyone participates.	
Student 2: **Secretary**	Write out the role-play with help from the team. Make sure there is a part for everyone.	
Student 3: **Director**	Direct the role-play.	
Students 4/5: **Spokespeople**	Introduce the role-play.	

2. Choose an accident or illness. Write down the injured or sick person's symptoms. Who is the patient in your group? What is his or her name in the role-play?

3. Write a conversation with a 911 operator.

4. Write a conversation with a doctor. Write a medicine label with directions. In the conversation, the doctor gives a prescription.

5. Write a conversation with a family member of the patient.

6. Put the conversations together.

7. Present the role-play to the class.

EXPLORER GRACE GOBBO

Searching for Medicinal Plants

"It's so rewarding to help people understand the value of conservation, sustainable agriculture, and holistic remedies."
—Grace Gobbo

A. A remedy is something we use when we are sick. Match the remedy to the illness.

1. Drink water very fast.

2. Take honey.

3. Drink homemade ginger tea.

4. Put heat on the belly.

a. cough

b. stomachache

c. hiccups

d. headaches

B. **PREDICT** Read the title of the paragraph. What do you think it is about? Tell a group.

a. I think the story is about plants that make you sick.

b. I think the story is about plants used to help sick people.

c. I think the story is about drug companies who make medicine from plants.

d. I think the story is about expensive medicine.

C. **Read about Grace Gobbo.**

Plants and Medicine

Grace Gobbo wants to help sick people. She lives in Tanzania. Medicine is very expensive there. Traditional healers help people who are ill. Traditional healers find less expensive medicines for chest problems, stomachaches, coughs, and many other illnesses and symptoms. These medicines come from plants in the rainforest. Grace wants to share these medicines with her people. She believes people in her country should be healthy, and they shouldn't pay a lot of money for medicine.

D. **ANALYZE** **Study the paragraph and discover new words. Answer the questions.**

1. A healer is someone who helps people when they are sick, but they are not always doctors or nurses. What do *traditional healers* do?

   a. They use plants to help sick people.

   b. They talk to people about the government.

   c. They buy medicine at a pharmacy to help people.

2. A forest is a group of trees. What do you think a *rain*forest is? Which picture is probably a rainforest and why do you think so?

3. Grace wants to *share* the medicine with her people. What do you think *share* means and what does she want to do? Read the next sentences in the paragraph to help you.

   a. She wants to buy medicines for her people.

   b. She wants to sell medicines to make money.

   c. She wants to teach people about the medicines.

E. **In a group, make a list of medicines you buy for stomachaches, colds, or coughs. Estimate the cost of each item on the list. Then, share your list with the class.**

F. **CREATE** **In a group, describe a home remedy.**

Working On It

Three mine repair workers stand for a
portrait inside a huge dipper in Utah.

UNIT OUTCOMES

- ☐ Identify common occupations
- ☐ Interpret job information
- ☐ Write your job history
- ☐ Perform a job interview
- ☐ Interpret performance reviews

Look at the photo and answer the questions.

1. What do you see in the picture?
2. What are they wearing?
3. What kind of job do the workers have?

LESSON **1** What's your job?

GOAL ▪ Identify common occupations

A. **IDENTIFY** Write the jobs from the box under the pictures.

| teller | nurse | office worker | server | mechanic |

Alan
1. _____server_____

Michelle
2. _____

Tony
3. _____

Huong
4. _____

Isabel
5. _____

B. **Practice the conversations. Then, ask questions about the people above.**

Student A: What is Tony's job?

Student B: He is a mechanic.

Student B: What does Tony do?

Student A: He's a mechanic.

C. **Study the pictures with your classmates and teacher.**

1. cook/chef

2. server

3. custodian

4. cashier

5. secretary

6. teacher

D. **CLASSIFY** **Write the job titles from Exercise C in the correct column.**

Restaurant	School
cook/chef	secretary

E. **Listen to each conversation. Circle the correct job title.**

CD 2
TR 30-33

1. secretary	teacher	custodian
2. cashier	server	cook
3. secretary	teacher	custodian
4. cashier	server	cook

F. Study the charts with your classmates and teacher.

Simple Present		
Subject	**Verb**	**Example sentence**
I, You, We, They	work	I **work** in an office.
He, She, It	works	He **works** in a restaurant.

Negative Simple Present			
Subject	**Negative**	**Verb**	**Example sentence**
I, You, We, They	do not (don't)	work	I **don't work** in an office. You **don't work** in a restaurant.
He, She, It	does not (doesn't)		He **doesn't work** in a school. She **doesn't work** in a hospital.

G. Look at the jobs in Exercise C. Ask and answer questions about each job.

Student A: What does he do? (Point to the cook.)
Student B: He is a <u>cook</u>.
Student A: He works <u>in a school</u>, right?
Student B: No, he doesn't work <u>in a school</u>. He works <u>in a restaurant</u>.

INTONATION
Put emphasis on requested information and on corrected information. He works IN A SCHOOL, right? No, he doesn't work IN A SCHOOL. He works IN A RESTAURANT.

H. **SURVEY** Talk to three classmates. Complete the chart. Then, report to a group.

Huong is a nurse. She works in a hospital.

Name	What do you do?	Where do you work?
Huong	nurse	hospital

LESSON **2** Job hunting

GOAL ■ Interpret job information

A. INTERPRET Read the classified ads and discuss them with your teacher.

Cook Needed

Regal Diner

2 yrs exp, f/t or p/t,
gd bnfts, appl avail.
$10/hr. Call 555-7454 or
apply in person at 232
W. Broadway M-F, 8-6

BBQ Madness

Position : Cook
Location : 8258 River Road
Hourly Rate : $12
Type : full-time

Summary:
Responsible for preparing foods and performing all other
responsibilities as directed by management. 1 year experience.

Essential Functions:
• Read and follow recipes
• Clean equipment
• Operate kitchen equipment

Benefits
• 1 week vacation annually
• medical insurance

Apply

B. COMPARE Write the information in the chart.

	Regal Diner	BBQ Madness
Position / Job Title	*cook*	*cook*
Location		
Pay / Wages / Salary		
Full- or Part-time?		
Benefits		
Experience		

C. Listen to the conversations. Check (✓) the correct benefits.

CD 2
TR 34-36

1. Listen to Roberto and his boss. Check (✓) the benefit.

☐ vacation ☐ sick leave ☐ insurance

2. Listen to Anya and her supervisor. Check (✓) the benefit.

☐ vacation ☐ sick leave ☐ insurance

3. Listen to Steve and his manager. Check (✓) the benefit.

☐ vacation ☐ sick leave ☐ insurance

D. EVALUATE Study the information in the chart about jobs.

Position	Experience	Full-time / Part-time	Benefits (Yes/No)	Pay
1. Nurse	2 years	F/T	Yes	$22/hr
2. Server	No	P/T	No	$10/hr + tips
3. Driver	No	F/T or P/T	Yes	$18/hr
4. Cashier	No	P/T	No	$8/hr
5. Mechanic	No	F/T	Yes	$12/hr

E. Practice the conversation and then create new conversations with information from the chart.

Applicant:	I am interested in the <u>nurse</u> position.
Manager:	Great. Do you have any questions?
Applicant:	Yes. Is the position full-time or part-time?
Manager:	It's <u>full-time</u>. The pay is <u>$22 an hour</u>.
Applicant:	And benefits?
Manager:	<u>Yes, there are benefits.</u>
Applicant:	Thank you for the information. I will apply online.

> **YES / NO**
> Yes, there are benefits.
> No, there are no benefits.

🎧 **F.** Listen and write the missing words.

CD 2
TR 37

> We need a _____ for our restaurant in San Francisco. The salary is _____ an hour. You need _____ years experience for this job. This is a full-time position with benefits. We offer _____ and a two-week _____ every year. Apply in person at 3500 West Arbor Place, San Francisco, California.

G. Read about Silvia, Anh, and Amal.

Silvia

Skills:

She can drive.

She can speak English.

She can speak Spanish.

She can work at night.

Needs:

She needs a part-time job.

Anh

Skills:

She can't drive.

She can speak English.

She can't work at night.

She can't speak Spanish.

Needs:

She needs a part-time job.

Amal

Skills:

He can drive.

He can speak English.

He can't speak Spanish.

He can work at night.

Needs:

He needs a full-time job.

H. **ANALYZE** Work in a group. Look at the information in Exercise D. Write the jobs that are good for Silvia, Anh, and Amal.

Silvia	Anh	Amal

I. **CREATE** In a group, make a classified ad for the Internet. Use another sheet of paper. Include the information below. See Exercise A for an example.

business name	job title	location	hourly rate
full- or part-time	experience needed	benefit information	

J. Look in the newspaper or on the Internet to find a job you want. Tell the class about the job.

LESSON ③ What was your job before?

GOAL ▧ Write your job history

A. PREDICT Look at the picture. What is Francisco's job? Does he work inside or outside? Then, read about Francisco.

My name is Francisco. I'm from Guatemala. Now, I work in the United States. I'm a mail carrier. I deliver mail to about two hundred houses every day. I started my job in July of 2010. Before I moved to the United States, I was a cook from March 2005 to July 2010. I cooked hamburgers and french fries in a fast-food restaurant.

B. SUMMARIZE Answer the questions in complete sentences and then tell a summary to a partner.

1. Where is Francisco from? _____

2. What is his job now? _____

3. What does he do in his job? _____

4. When did he start his job? _____

5. What was his job in Guatemala? _____

6. Where did he work in Guatemala? _____

C. Complete the job history for Francisco.

Job History				
POSITION	**COMPANY**	**FROM**	**TO**	**DUTIES (Responsibilities)**
Mail carrier	US Government			
	Mr. Burger			
Server	La Cantina	March 2002	March 2005	served customers

D. Study the charts with your classmates and teacher.

Simple Past: Regular Verbs			
Subject	**Base verb + *ed***		**Example sentence**
I, You, He, She, It, We, They	cleaned	tables	I **cleaned** tables.
	cooked	hamburgers	You **cooked** hamburgers.
	prepared	breakfast	He **prepared** breakfast.
	delivered	packages	She **delivered** packages.
	counted	the money	I **counted** the money.
	helped	other workers	We **helped** other workers.
	moved	to the United States	They **moved** to the United States.

Simple Past: *Be*			
Subject	***Be***		**Example sentence**
I, He, She, It	was	a mail carrier	I **was** a mail carrier.
We, You, They	were	happy	You **were** happy.

E. Complete each sentence with the correct form of the word in parentheses.

1. Anya was an office worker.
   She ___typed___ (type) letters.

2. Ernesto was a delivery person.
   He _____ (deliver) packages.

3. David was a cashier.
   He _____ (count) money.

4. Anita was a nurse.
   She _____ (help) the doctors.

5. Eva and Anya were teachers.
   They _____ (work) in a school.

6. Derek was a salesperson.
   He _____ (talk) to customers.

7. So was a mechanic.
   He _____ (fix) cars.

8. Mary was a cook.
   She _____ (prepare) lunch.

9. Agatha was a manager.
   She _____ (supervise) the other workers.

10. I was a _____.
    I _____.

F. **Practice the conversation with your partner. Then, make new conversations using the information below.**

Miyuki: What was your last job?

Anya: I was <u>an office worker</u>.

Miyuki: What did you do as <u>an office worker</u>?

Anya: I <u>typed letters</u>.

Miyuki: What do you do now?

Anya: I am <u>a student</u>. I <u>study English</u>.

Before

1. office worker / type letters

2. teacher / help students

3. mechanic / fix cars

4. mail carrier / deliver letters

5. cook / cook hamburgers

6. busboy / clean tables

Now

student / study English

writer / write books

driver / drive a taxi

salesperson / sell computers

server / serve food

cashier / count money

G. **Listen and complete the job history. Then, practice the conversation in Exercise F again with the new information.**

CD 2
TR 38

POSITION	COMPANY	FROM	TO	DUTIES (Responsibilities)
Nurse	Arch Memorial Hospital	February 2012	Present	
Office worker	Arch Memorial Hospital	May 2009	February 2012	
Receptionist	Arch Memorial Hospital	January 2006	May 2009	

H. **APPLY** **Complete the job history for yourself.**

POSITION	COMPANY	FROM	TO	DUTIES (Responsibilities)

I. **Get a job application from a business or find one on the Internet. How much can you complete? Can you complete the job history section?**

LESSON **4** **A job interview**

GOAL ◻ Perform a job interview

A. Look at the pictures. What is good at a job interview? What is not good?

chewing gum

checking texts

firm handshake

eye contact

good posture

bright clothing

B. **CLASSIFY** Use the words above to complete the chart. Then, add your own ideas.

Good at a job interview	Not good at a job interview
firm handshake	chewing gum

C. Read the chart.

Questions with *Can*				
Can	**Subject**	**Base verb**	**Example questions**	**Example answers**
Can	I	ask answer	Can I ask you a question? Can you answer a few questions?	Yes, of course. Absolutely.
	you	work follow speak	Can you work on weekends? Can you follow directions? Can you speak English well?	No, I'm sorry. I can't. Yes, I can. I believe so. I am studying in school.

D. **PREDICT** Complete with a question from the chart. Then, listen for the correct answer.

CD 2
TR 39-41

1. **Applicant:** _____?

   Interviewer: Yes, please do.

   Applicant: What are the benefits?

2. **Interviewer:** _____?

   Applicant: Yes, on Saturday, but not on Sunday.

   Interviewer: OK, that's good to know.

3. **Interviewer:** _____?

   Applicant: I think I do. I am studying in school.

   Interviewer: Yes, I think you do, too. I just want to make sure.

E. **CLARIFY** Match each question with a clarification question. Draw lines.

1. What is your name?
2. What do you do?
3. Do you have experience?
4. Can you work eight hours?
5. Can you work on Saturdays?

a. Experience for this job?
b. My name?
c. Full-time?
d. On the weekends?
e. What is my job now?

INTONATION

Clarification Questions

My name?

On the weekends?

F. Look at the picture. Who is Miyuki talking to? What is she doing? Then, study the phrases with your teacher. What are your strengths?

I communicate well.	I am a hard worker.
I am punctual.	I listen and follow directions well.

G. **CONTRAST** Write the phrases from Exercise F in the chart next to the weakness.

Strengths	Weaknesses
	Sometimes, I'm late.
	I like to take a lot of breaks.
	I don't always listen.
	Sometimes people don't understand me.

H. **INTERPRET** Read the paragraphs about Mary and Neda.

> **SYNONYMS**
> employee = worker

Mary's Work Inventory

I am a good employee.* I work hard. Sometimes I'm late. I always listen and follow directions well. I am learning English. Sometimes people don't understand me. I want to be a great employee. I need to communicate well and to come to work on time.

Neda's School Inventory

I don't work. I go to school. I am punctual. I don't always listen well. I am learning English. Sometimes people don't understand me. Sometimes I don't do my homework. I want to be a great student. I need to communicate well and do my homework every day.

I. **APPLY** Write your own Work or School Inventory on another sheet of paper. Use Exercise H as an example.

J. Write and practice a job interview. Use the information from this lesson to help you with the questions.

LESSON 5 He's a good worker

A. Look at Fernando's evaluation. What is good? What is a problem?

EVALUATION FORM

DATE: May 4, 2016
COMPANY: Paul's Radio and CD
NAME: Fernando Gaspar
POSITION: Sales Clerk
SUPERVISOR: Leticia Garcia

Punctuality:
Superior   Good   (Needs improvement)

Appearance (professional dress and grooming):
(Superior)   Good   Needs improvement

Communication Skills:
Superior   (Good)   Needs improvement

Product Knowledge:
Superior   (Good)   Needs improvement

Fernando is a good employee. I worked with him for eight hours on April 28 to evaluate his performance. He talked with the customers well. He was ten minutes late to work. This is a problem. He said he had a problem with his car. Fernando is a good salesperson and he has very good knowledge of the product.

SIGNED: *Leticia Garcia*

B. **EVALUATE** Look at the evaluation and answer the questions.

1. Where does Fernando work? _____

2. What is his supervisor's name? _____

3. What does Fernando do well? _____

4. What does he do very well? _____

5. What does he need to improve? _____

C. Study the charts with your classmates and teacher.

Simple Present: *Be*			
Subject	**Be**		**Example sentence**
I	am		I **am** always early.
He, She, It	is	early late on time punctual	He **is** sometimes late. She **is** a good worker.
We, You, They	are		We **are** often early. You **are** never on time. They **are** always punctual.

Adverbs of Frequency

0%		50%		100%
never	rarely	sometimes	usually	always

Simple Past: *Be*			
Subject	**Be**		**Example sentence**
I, He, She, It	was	early late	I **was** early yesterday. He **was** often late. She **was** always a good worker.
We, You, They	were	on time punctual	We **were** early on Saturday. You **were** on time today. They **were** never punctual.

D. Complete the sentences with the correct form of *be*.

1. Mario and Alberto _____*were*_____ early to work yesterday.

2. I _____ never on time last year, but now I _____ always on time.

3. She _____ punctual every day last year.

4. We come to work on time every day. We _____ rarely late.

5. You _____ a good worker. You always work well with customers.

E. **ANALYZE** Read about Alberto. Underline the *be* verbs.

Alberto is a good worker. He works at night. He is punctual. The customers love him. Last night, Alberto was late for work. He had a problem with his car. His car is old. He called a tow truck with his cell phone and the tow truck was late.

🎧 **F.** **Listen to John's evaluation. Circle the correct rating** (*Needs Improvement,* *Good,* **or** *Superior*).

EVALUATION FORM

DATE: May 4, 2016
COMPANY: Paul's Radio and CD
NAME: John Perkins
POSITION: Sales Clerk
SUPERVISOR: Leticia Garcia

Punctuality:

Superior   Good   Needs improvement

Appearance (professional dress and grooming):

Superior   Good   Needs improvement

Communication Skills:

Superior   Good   Needs improvement

Product Knowledge:

Superior   Good   Needs improvement

Comments:

I worked with John for four hours. He is new. He needs to learn more
about the product. He doesn't dress well and he needs to comb
his hair. He said he was tired today. I think he has three jobs.
This is a problem. John communicates well with the customers.

Signed: *Leticia Garcia*

G. **RANK** **In a group, rank the areas 1–4. Number 1 is the most important.**

_____ Punctuality

_____ Appearance

_____ Communication

_____ Product Knowledge

► **How did you hear about this job?**

Before You Watch

A. **Look at the picture. Complete each sentence.**

1. Hector is at a

   _____.

2. Mr. Patel is reading Hector's

   _____.

3. He is going to ask about Hector's

   _____.

While You Watch

B. ► **Watch the video. Read the statements. Write T for *True* or F for *False*.**

1. Hector does not have an appointment for an interview.   __F__

2. Mr. Patel is the store manager.   _____

3. Hector saw an ad for the job.   _____

4. Hector can work in the mornings and evenings.   _____

5. Mr. Patel hires Hector.   _____

Check Your Understanding

C. **Complete the dialog. Use the words in the box.**

answered	~~application~~	assistant	did	experience	history

Mr. Patel: Let's take it one step at a time . . . Did you bring an (1) _____application_____?

Hector: Yes, here it is. I know I don't have very much (2) _____.

Mr. Patel: Never mind that. Tell me about your work (3) _____. What was your last job?

Hector: I was an . . . (4) _____.

Mr. Patel: And what was it that you (5) _____ as an "assistant"?

Hector: I (6) _____ the phones and took messages.

Review

A. Write the name of the job below each picture.

1. _____   2. _____   3. _____

B. Read the ads and complete the chart below.

1.
Office Assistant
f/t, gd bnfts,
4 yrs exp nec,
$17/hr,
Call 555-2298.

2.
Restaurant Manager
p/t, restaurant exp nec,
$14/hr, no bnfts,
Apply in person
at 2222 E. Fourth St.
8am to 12pm, M-F.

3.
Delivery Person
p/t, work 7 days, no bnfts,
$8/hr, no exp, will train,
current driver's license,
speak Eng. and Span.
Call 555-5477.

4.
CARPENTER
f/t, good bnfts, no exp,
$22 an hour,
must be 18 yrs. old.
Apply in person at
3333 W. Broadway
during office hours.

5.
Mechanic
Mike's Garage
f/t, night shift,
$12/hour, no exp nec,
will train, bnfts,
Call 555-7469.

Position	Experience	F/T or P/T	Benefits	Pay
1.				
2.				
3.				
4.				
5.				

C. Write a classified ad for a receptionist.

Company: _____

Position: _____

Location: _____

Hourly Rate: _____

Type: _____

Benefits: _____

D. Complete the paragraph with the past tense form of the verbs in parentheses.

In 2005, Jarek was a carpenter. He _____ (construct) homes for Builders Plus Company. In 2007, Jarek was a custodian. He _____ (clean) the offices for Clean Sweep Maintenance Company. In 2010, Jarek was a server. He _____ (talk) to customers at the Polish Café. Now Jarek is a teacher. He helps students at Jefferson Adult School.

E. Complete the job history for Jarek.

POSITION	COMPANY	FROM	TO	DUTIES (Responsibilities)

F. Label the pictures and circle *good* or *bad* for a job interview.

good / bad

1. ch _____ _____

good / bad

2. g _____ _____

good / bad

3. f _____ _____

good / bad

4. ch _____ _____

good / bad

5. br _____ _____

good / bad

6. e _____ _____

G. Complete the paragraph with the correct form of the verbs from the box. Choose the present or past tense. You will use one of the verbs two times.

be	move	work	live	help	deliver	like

Francisco _____ in Guatemala before he _____ to California. In Guatemala, he _____ a cook at a small fast-food restaurant. He _____ in the kitchen. He _____ 14 hours every day. Now, he _____ a mail carrier in California. He _____ letters and packages. He _____ his new job very much.

H. Match the words and definitions. Draw lines.

1. punctuality

2. communicate

3. appearance

a. clothing and posture

b. on time

c. talk

TEAM PROJECT ✔ Get a new job

In this project, you will prepare one member of your team to complete the process for getting a job.

1. **COLLABORATE** Form a team with four or five students. In your team, you need:

Position	Job description	Student name
Student 1: **Team Leader**	Check that everyone speaks English. Check that everyone participates.	
Student 2: **Writer**	With help from the team, write a classified ad, a job history, and a job evaluation.	
Student 3: **Director**	With help from the team, write and direct an interview.	
Students 4/5: **Spokespeople**	With help from the team, organize a presentation to give to the class.	

2. Choose one member of your team to look for a new job. Decide on a position he or she is interested in.

3. Write a classified ad describing the position.

4. Write a real or imaginary job history for the person looking for a job.

5. Write an imaginary job evaluation from an old job.

6. Write a conversation of a job interview and practice the conversation.

7. As a team, make a presentation of all the previous steps and perform the conversation.

EXPLORER THOMAS CULHANE

Solar Power Provider

"This is not a new or exotic technology. I believe Egypt could solve at least half its energy needs by immediately going solar."
—Thomas Taha Rassam Culhane

A. **Look at the picture. Read about Thomas Culhane's organization.**

a. Solar C3ITIES is an organization co-founded by Thomas Culhane.

b. It makes power from the sun.

c. It helps people heat water.

d. It works with poor people all over the world.

> Thomas Culhane also teaches people to build passive solar heated food-waste-to-fuel-and-fertilizer biodigesters.

B. **PREDICT** **The words below are in the reading about Thomas Culhane. Match the letter of the definition to the word.**

_____ solar   a. to make something

_____ build   b. a machine to make water hot

_____ co-founder   c. what you do when something is funny

_____ water heater   d. from the sun

_____ laugh   e. someone who started something with another person

C. On another sheet of paper, combine the sentences in Exercise A into a paragraph.

D. Read about Thomas Culhane and his organization.

> **Solar for the Poor**
>
> Thomas Culhane is a National Geographic Explorer and the co-founder of Solar C3ITIES. He helps poor people all over the world. They need hot and cold water in their homes. Thomas says that poor people have skills. They are carpenters, plumbers, glassworkers, etc. Thomas helps them build water heaters that are powered by the sun. Before working in countries like Egypt, Thomas was a teacher. He was also a researcher at Harvard University. In 1976, Thomas made people laugh as a job. He was a clown for the Ringling Brothers Circus.

E. **INTERACT** Find answers in the paragraph.

1. Do you think Thomas builds the water heaters by himself? Find one or two words that help you answer the question.

   _____

2. Is Thomas a clown now in the Ringling Brothers Circus? Find one or two words that help you answer the question.

   _____

3. What are examples of the *skills* Thomas is talking about.

   _____

F. **APPLY** Why do people need hot and cold water? In a group, make a list.

to wash clothes _____

_____

_____

_____

_____

Lifelong Learning and Review

Johnny Thomsen is a musician. He plays at many types of community gatherings. He practices playing his instruments every day.

UNIT OUTCOMES

- [ ] Evaluate study habits
- [ ] Organize study
- [ ] Identify learning opportunities
- [ ] Identify vocational preferences
- [ ] Develop goals

Look at the photo and answer the questions.

1. What does Johnny Thomsen do?
2. Where does he play?
3. When does he practice?

GOAL ▪ Evaluate study habits

A. **PREDICT** Look at the picture. What is Nubar doing? Why? Then, read about Nubar.

Nubar is a good ESL student at Franklin Adult School. He comes to school every day. He also studies at home. Some students practice English at work. Others practice English with their families. Nubar learns two or three new words a day at home. Sometimes Nubar watches TV or listens to the radio.

B. **CLASSIFY** In a group, write different ways to study or practice English.

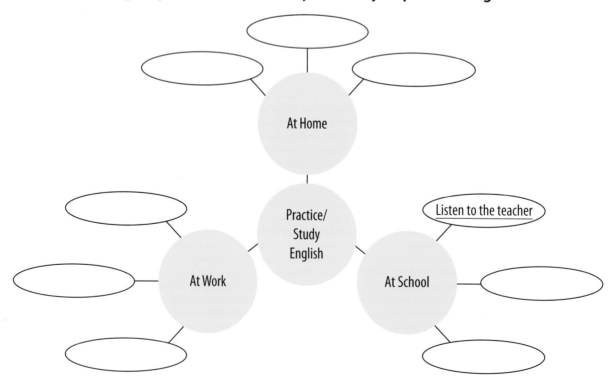

C. Study the charts with your classmates and teacher.

Regular Past Tense Verbs	
Base	Simple past
study	studied
participate	participated
help	helped
listen	listened
watch	watched
practice	practiced
learn	learned

Irregular Past Tense Verbs	
Base	Simple past
come	came
see	saw
write	wrote
speak	spoke
read	read
teach	taught

D. Rewrite the sentences in the past tense. Then, use the sentences to write a paragraph in your notebook.

1. Nubar comes to class every day.

   Nubar came to class every day. _____

2. Nubar studies at home.

   _____

3. Some students practice at work.

   _____

4. Some students watch TV or listen to the radio.

   _____

5. Nubar reads for one or two hours a day at home.

   _____

E. Listen to Angela talk about her study skills. Check (✓) the things she did to study.

CD 2
TR 43

☐ came to class every day

☐ came to class on time

☐ helped other students

☐ learned new words every day

☐ listened to the radio

☐ participated in class

☐ practiced at work

☐ studied at home

☐ taught other students

☐ watched TV

F. **EVALUATE** Answer the questions about this course. Check (✓) the correct answer.

Study Habits Questionnaire

1. How often did you come to class?
   - ☐ a. most of the time
   - ☐ b. more than 50%
   - ☐ c. less than 50%

2. Did you come to class on time?
   - ☐ a. most of the time
   - ☐ b. more than 50%
   - ☐ c. less than 50%

3. How much did you study at home each week?
   - ☐ a. more than 10 hours
   - ☐ b. 5–10 hours
   - ☐ c. less than 5 hours

4. Did you speak English in class and participate?
   - ☐ a. most of the time
   - ☐ b. more than 50%
   - ☐ c. less than 50%

5. Did you teach and help other students in class?
   - ☐ a. a lot
   - ☐ b. a little
   - ☐ c. never

6. Did you listen to the radio in English?
   - ☐ a. a lot
   - ☐ b. a little
   - ☐ c. never

7. Did you watch TV in English?
   - ☐ a. a lot
   - ☐ b. a little
   - ☐ c. never

8. Did you ask the teacher or other students questions when you didn't understand?
   - ☐ a. a lot
   - ☐ b. a little
   - ☐ c. never

How many *a* answers, *b* answers, and *c* answers do you have?

# of *a* answers_____	# of *b* answers_____	# of *c* answers_____

Do the math below.

of *a* answers x 3 = _____
of *b* answers x 2 = _____
of *c* answers x 1 = _____
Total = _____

Score: **20–24** Super – You have great study habits!

Score: **16–19** Good – You have great study habits.

Score: **Under 16** – You need to change your study habits.

LESSON **2** Staying organized

GOAL ■ Organize study

A. Talk about the pictures with your classmates and teacher.

1. <u>listening</u>

2. _____

SIMPLE PRESENT

I like . . .

He / She likes . . .

3. _____

4. _____

5. _____

FOR RENT

2 bed, 3 bath apt.
a/c, elect. pd.
Call Margaret for
more information–
555-2672.

6. _____

7. _____

8. _____

B. What do you learn in English class? Write a word from the box for each picture above.

grammar	~~listening~~	speaking	writing
life skills	reading	teamwork	vocabulary

C. **COLLABORATE** In a group, think of other things you learn in English class.

_____   _____

_____   _____

D. **APPLY** Complete the chart about yourself. Use the words from Exercise B.

Things I do well	Things I need help with

E. Make a study guide. Make one page for each skill from Exercise B and add a page for a journal.

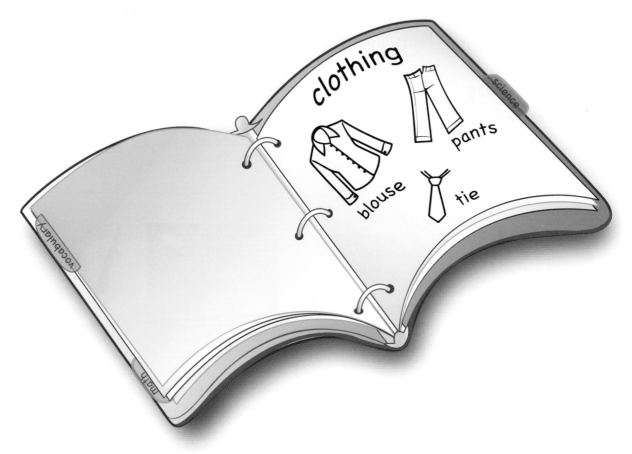

F. Write new words in the Vocabulary page. List one or two new words you learned from each unit in this book.

G. In a group, write on the Listening page ways you can practice listening outside of class.

H. **REFLECT** On the Grammar page, write the name of the grammar tenses you have learned in this book. Use pages 214–219 to help you with this.

> **CAN**
>
> I **can** listen to the radio.
> You **can** listen to …
> He/She **can** listen to …
> We **can** listen to …
> They **can** listen to …

I. **What are life skills? Read the definition.**

Every lesson in this book teaches a life skill. Life skills are what we do often every day, like reading a bus schedule or making a doctor's appointment.

J. **Listen and write the life skills you hear in the conversation. Then, write them on your study guide page for Life Skills.**

_____

_____

_____

K. **Read the journal notes.**

New Words: checkout, counter, cough
Skill: I practiced in the supermarket. "Where is the medicine?"
Book: I reviewed pages 10–15 in the textbook from last semester.
Listening: TV—I watched Channel 20 for ten minutes at 7a.m.
Writing: I wrote in my journal.

L. **CREATE** **What did you do today to help you practice English? Write the information here and in your study guide.**

M. **Now that you have made a study guide, make a notebook. Put each page of the study guide in a section of your notebook.**

LESSON 3 Schools in the United States

GOAL ■ Identify learning opportunities

A. ANALYZE Read the diagram with your classmates and teacher.

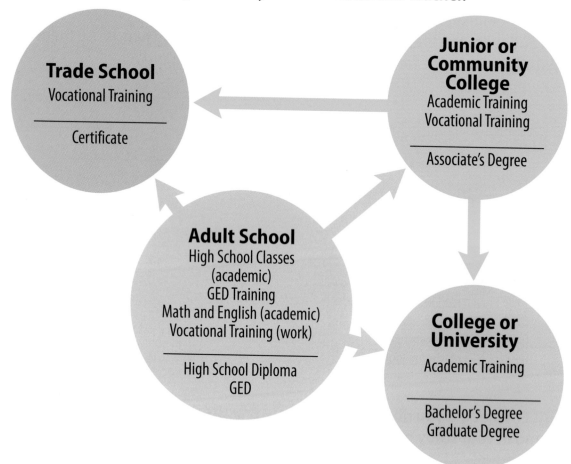

B. INTERPRET Complete the chart about learning opportunities.

School	Degree or diploma
Adult School	
Trade School	
Junior or Community College	
College or University	

C. **PREDICT** Read the information about the students. What kind of education do you think they need?

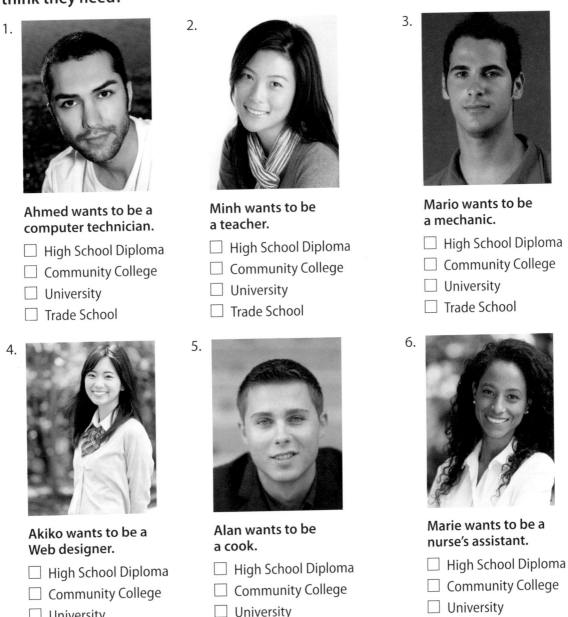

1.

Ahmed wants to be a computer technician.

☐ High School Diploma
☐ Community College
☐ University
☐ Trade School

2.

Minh wants to be a teacher.

☐ High School Diploma
☐ Community College
☐ University
☐ Trade School

3.

Mario wants to be a mechanic.

☐ High School Diploma
☐ Community College
☐ University
☐ Trade School

4.

Akiko wants to be a Web designer.

☐ High School Diploma
☐ Community College
☐ University
☐ Trade School

5.

Alan wants to be a cook.

☐ High School Diploma
☐ Community College
☐ University
☐ Trade School

6.

Marie wants to be a nurse's assistant.

☐ High School Diploma
☐ Community College
☐ University
☐ Trade School

D. Listen to the conversations and check the correct information in Exercise C.

CD 2
TR 45-50

SHOULD
I **should** go to college.
You **should** go …
He/She **should** go …
We **should** go …
They **should** go …

E. Practice the conversation with a partner. Ask about the students in Exercise C.

Student A: Where should Ahmed go to school after the adult school?

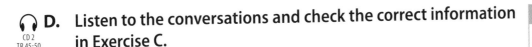

Student B: He should go to a trade school.

Lesson 3   193

F. Look at the pictures. What are the people doing? Then, in a group, make a list of three or four places you can go to for advice about learning opportunities.

_____

_____

_____

_____

_____

G. **APPLY** What do you want to do after adult school? Fill in the boxes and talk to a partner.

| Adult School | → | _____ | → | _____ |

H. What books or Internet sites can help you with your educational choices? Tell the class.

GOAL ▢ Identify vocational preferences

A. PREDICT Read the information about the students. Circle the job that you think is the best for each one.

Position	Job
1. Roberto likes to study. He likes school. He likes history.	teacher mechanic doctor
2. Eva likes to help people. She likes to talk to people. She likes to study.	gardener nurse receptionist
3. Duong likes to work with his hands. He likes to fix things. He likes cars.	mechanic manager salesperson

B. Listen to the conversations. Check your predictions in Exercise A.

CD 2
TR 51-53

C. Talk to a partner. List three things your partner likes to do.

_____ _____ _____

D. Study the charts with your classmates and teacher.

Verb + Infinitive			
Subject	**Verb**	**Infinitive**	**Example sentence**
I, You, We, They	like want need	to read to travel to work to talk to handle to study	I like **to read**. You want **to travel**. We need **to work** alone. They like **to talk** on the phone.
He, She, It	likes wants needs		He likes **to handle** money. She wants **to study**.

Verb + Noun			
Subject	**Verb**	**Noun**	**Example sentence**
I, You, We, They	like want need	cars computer books school food	I like **cars**. You want a **computer**. We need **books**. They like **school**.
He, She, It	likes wants needs		He likes **computers**. She wants **food**.

E. Complete each sentence with the correct form of the verb in parentheses.

1. They like _____ (work) outside.

2. He wants _____ (study) at school every day.

3. She needs _____ (make) money right now.

4. They want _____ (handle) money.

5. I want _____ (learn) English.

6. We like _____ (read) books.

7. I like _____ (talk) on the telephone.

8. You want _____ (work) at the university.

F. Talk to a different partner than in Exercise C. List three things your partner likes to do. Report to a group.

_____ _____ _____

G. **PLAN** A counselor is going to ask you questions to help you with your future plans. Answer the questions about yourself. Check (✓) *Yes* or *No*.

Personal Inventory

	Yes	No
1. Do you have a high school diploma?	☐	☐
2. Do you have good study skills?	☐	☐
3. Do you have experience?	☐	☐
4. Do you like technology (computers, machines)?	☐	☐
5. Do you like to do the same thing every day?	☐	☐
6. Do you like to handle money?	☐	☐
7. Do you like to read?	☐	☐
8. Do you like to study and to learn new things?	☐	☐
9. Do you like to listen to people?	☐	☐
10. Do you like to talk on the phone?	☐	☐
11. Do you like to travel?	☐	☐
12. Do you like to work with other people?	☐	☐
13. Do you like to work alone?	☐	☐
14. Do you like to work at night?	☐	☐
15. Do you like to work in the daytime?	☐	☐
16. Do you like to work with your hands?	☐	☐
17. Do you like your job?	☐	☐
18. Do you work now?	☐	☐
19. Do you have goals for the future?	☐	☐

H. Discuss your answers in a group.

LESSON **5** **Making goals**

GOAL ◼ Develop goals

A. Read Nubar's journal entry. Answer the questions about his study goals.

> September 5
>
>   I have many study goals for the next month. I am going to read
> the newspaper, listen to the radio, and talk to people in English
> every day. I am also going to study four pages from my textbook
> every night for 30 minutes in my bedroom.

1. When is Nubar going to study? _____

2. Where is Nubar going to study? _____

3. What is he going to study? _____

4. How long is he going to study? _____

B. Look at the clocks. Then, listen to Nubar talk about his plans. Write what he is going to do next to the clocks. Use the phrases from the box.

CD 2
TR 54

listen to the radio	read the newspaper	write in a journal
review vocabulary	study the textbook	

From ⏰ to ⏰ _____

From ⏰ to ⏰ _____

From ⏰ to ⏰ _____

From ⏰ to ⏰ _____

198 Unit 8

C. **Study the chart with your classmates and teacher.**

Future with *Going to*			
Subject	*Going to*	**Base verb**	**Example sentence**
I	am going to (I'm going to)	learn	I **am going to** learn English.
You, We, They	are going to (you're/we're/they're going to)	listen practice read	We **are going to** practice English.
He, She, It	is going to (he's/she's going to)	speak study write	She **is going to** speak English.

Use *going to* for future plans that can change.

D. **Write sentences about Nubar's plans. Use the information from Exercise B.**

1. He is going to read the newspaper from 6:30 to 6:45.

2. _____

3. _____

4. _____

E. **PLAN** **What are your study plans? Write sentences and share them with a group.**

1. I _____

2. _____

3. _____

4. _____

F. Study another way to talk about future plans.

Future with *Will*			
Subject	***Will***	**Base**	**Example sentence**
I, You, He, She, It We, They	will	study work get married	I **will** study every day. She **will** work hard. They **will** get married.

Use *will* for future plans you are very sure about.

G. Read about Nubar's long-term goals.

June 12

    I have many goals for the future. Some of my goals will take a long time. I will study every day and get a high school diploma. After that, I will start college. I want to start in about three years. I also want to get married and have children sometime in the future. I will be a computer technician one day.

H. CLASSIFY Nubar wants to do many things. Write his goals in the chart.

Family goals	Educational goals	Work goals
He wants to get married.		

I. APPLY What are your family, educational, and work goals? Write them in the chart.

Family goals	Educational goals	Work goals

 # I have lots of different interests

Before You Watch

A. **Look at the picture. Complete each sentence.**

1. Hector is one of Mrs. Smith's

   _____.

2. Hector needs some

   _____.

3. Mrs. Smith is going to help him

   identify his _____.

While You Watch

B. ▶ **Watch the video. Complete the dialog. Use the words in the box.**

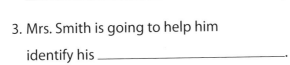

| gave | like | take | taking | took | ~~wanted~~ |

Hector: That's hard. I'm interested in lots of things. First, I (1) ___wanted___ to be an actor. Then, I wanted to be a teacher. Now, I'm not sure. I'm taking lots of different classes.

Mrs. Smith: Tell me, which classes did you (2) _____ last semester?

Hector: I (3) _____ a class in public speaking. That was fun.

Mrs. Smith: Oh, really? You (4) _____ to speak in public?

Hector: Let's just say I'm not shy. I (5) _____ a speech at least twice a week. And I took a class in world events, too.

Mrs. Smith: World events—very interesting. And what classes are you (6) _____ now?

Check Your Understanding

C. **Read the statements. Write T for *True* or F for *False*.**

1. Hector needs to choose his classes for the new semester. ____T____

2. He's not sure what classes he's going to take. _____

3. Last semester he took a class in journalism. _____

4. Hector likes to watch and listen to news programs. _____

Review

A. What are six things you did in this course to help you study English? Use the verbs from the box. Write sentences in the simple past tense.

participate	help	speak	ask	read	listen	~~come~~

1. I came to class on time.

2. _____

3. _____

4. _____

5. _____

6. _____

7. _____

B. Check (✓) the study skills.

☐ learn English ☐ get a high school diploma ☐ read

☐ go to college ☐ listen carefully ☐ write vocabulary words

☐ go to the supermarket ☐ ask questions ☐ eat a good breakfast

C. Write the things you can do well in class.

1. I can _____.

2. _____

3. _____

D. Ask a partner: *What can you do well in class?*

1. He can listen well. OR She can ask questions well. _____

2. _____

3. _____

4. _____

E. **Complete the paragraph with the words from the box.**

| degree | college | trade | diploma | GED | adult | certificate |

In the United States, adults can go to school in many different places. They can go to an
_____ school to learn English or to get a high school
_____ or _____. After adult school, students
can study at a _____ or a _____ school.
Students who go to a trade school get a _____ when they complete
the courses. Some students get a _____ from a university after
adult school.

F. **Complete the sentences with the correct form of the verb in parentheses.**

1. Javier likes _____ (study) in the afternoon.

2. The students _____ (want) to learn English.

3. I _____ (like) books.

4. She _____ (like) to read books.

5. We want _____ (go) to college.

6. You need _____ (speak) to a teacher.

7. Eva _____ (want) to see the homework.

8. He likes _____ (work) at night.

Review 203

G. Write sentences about Nam's future goals. Use *be going to*.

Nam

Now: Alton Adult School
Educational Goals: learn English, go to junior college
Work Goal: become a chef
Family Goal: buy a house

1. _____
2. _____
3. _____
4. _____

H. Write sentences about Gabriela's future goals. Use *will*.

Gabriela

Now: Alton Adult School
Educational Goals: get a high school diploma, go to a trade school
Work Goal: become a nurse
Family Goal: get married

1. _____
2. _____
3. _____
4. _____

✔ # Meet your goals

In this project, you will plan your study time on a calendar. You will also write out your goals and plans in two paragraphs. You will work with a team, and your team will help you polish your paragraphs and calendar. Then, you will present your paragraphs and calendar to the class.

1. Complete a calender for this month and next month. Write what days and what times you are going to do the following activities:

   - study your textbook
   - listen to the radio
   - read the newspaper
   - watch TV
   - review flash cards
   - write in your journal

2. **COLLABORATE** Discuss your plans with your team.

3. Write a paragraph about your goals on another piece of paper. Start your paragraph like this:

   > I have many goals. I'm going to be able to speak to Americans, understand TV programs in English, and find a job that requires English. First, ...

4. Write another paragraph about your plans for developing good study habits. Are you going to come to school every day? Are you going to arrive on time? What are other things you are going to do?

5. Ask members of your team to edit your paragraphs. Then, rewrite them.

6. Read your paragraphs to your team.

7. As a team, design a goal chart that you can each put in your home to remind you of your goals.

8. Present your calendar, paragraphs, and goal chart to the class.

EXPLORER JACK ANDRAKA

Making Discoveries

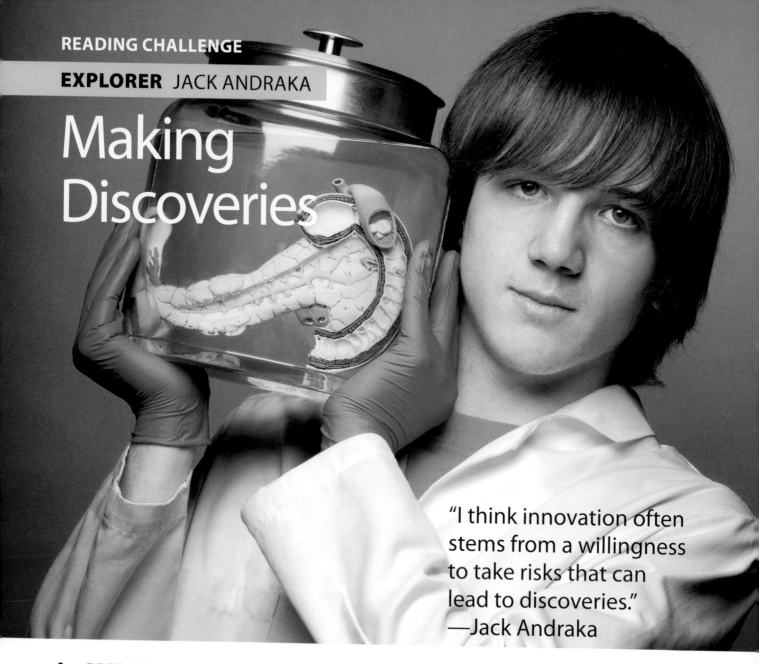

"I think innovation often stems from a willingness to take risks that can lead to discoveries."
—Jack Andraka

A. PREDICT Look at the picture and answer the questions.

1. How old is Jack in the picture?

   a. 17   b. 30   c. 50

2. What is his job?

   a. a mechanic   b. a cook   c. a researcher

B. Match the word with the definition.

1. researcher   a. a serious illness

2. discover   b. a person who looks for answers to questions or problems

3. cancer   c. life with friends and family

4. social life   d. to find something

C. **Read about Jack Andraka and his discovery.**

In 2015, Jack Andraka was 17 years old and a high school student. At the same time, he worked in a lab on important experiments, traveled, and shared his story with people all over the world. He is famous because, at 15 years old, he discovered a way to identify some forms of cancer. He is a researcher now. He continues to work and receive awards. In the future, he will study and learn more. He is learning to balance school, to work on his experiments, and to have a social life with speaking about his discovery with other researchers.

D. **CLASSIFY** **Complete the timeline about Jack's life.**

Past		Present	Future
2013	2015		
Discovered _____ _____ _____ _____ _____			

E. **CREATE** **Complete a timeline for you.**

Past	Present	Future

The Engaging Environmentalist

Before You Watch

A. Read the words and their definition. Check (✓) the ones you already know.

☐ **natural resource** thing we use that comes from nature	☐ **environment** the land, water, and air where people, animals, and plants live	☐ **movement** a group of people who work together because they believe the same thing	☐ **solution** the answer to a problem	☐ **school curriculum** courses that every student studies in school
☐ **advocacy** showing you believe in someone or something	☐ **mentorship** helping someone with less experience	☐ **pollution** damage to air, land, and water where people, animals, and plants live	☐ **extinction** when a type of animal or plant no longer lives	☐ **invest** to put time into something because you believe it is important

B. Complete the sentences. Use the words from Exercise A.

1. Teachers _____ a lot of time in their students' education.

2. Water is a _____ for every person, plant, and animal.

3. Our _____ needs more classes about the environment.

4. What is the best _____ for stopping air pollution?

5. Before its _____, there were more than 5 billion passenger pigeons on Earth.

C. Look at the map of Yucatan, Mexico. Circle the things you can find in the environment.

birds

cold temperatures

jungle

snow

fish

monkeys

trees

the ocean

mountains

hot temperatures

elephants

desert

While You Watch

D. Watch the video. Then read each question. Choose the correct answer.

1. Does *Ceiba Pentandra* have boats?

   a. Yes, it does.   b. No, it doesn't.

2. Does Maritza Morales Casanova have a dog?

   a. Yes, she does.   b. No, she doesn't.

3. Does *Ceiba Pentandra* have classrooms?

   a. Yes, it does.   b. No, it doesn't.

4. Do the children have video games at the park?

   a. Yes, they do.   b. No, they don't.

5. Does *Ceiba Pentandra* have a shopping mall?

   a. Yes, it does.   b. No, it doesn't.

6. Do the children have plants to take care of?

   a. Yes, they do.   b. No, they don't.

E. Watch the video again. What activities do you see the children doing? Check the correct answers.

_____ riding in a bus   _____ fishing for food   _____ painting pictures

_____ watering plants   _____ watching TV   _____ swimming in a pool

_____ riding bicycles   _____ playing games   _____ talking on a cell phone

F. Watch the video again. Read each sentence. Circle T for *True* or F for *False*.

1. Maritza Morales Casanova teaches children about the environment.   T   F

2. *Ceiba Pentandra* is a theme park in the United States.   T   F

3. The environment is a main subject in Mexico's schools.   T   F

4. The word for explorer in Spanish is *explorador*.   T   F

5. Maritza believes that the worst problem for the environment is pollution.   T   F

After You Watch

G. Write the correct type of environmental pollution under each picture.

light pollution	land pollution
noise pollution	water pollution
air pollution	

1. _____

2. _____

3. _____

4. _____

5. _____

H. **Read each sentence. Circle the environmental problem.**

1. Marisa can't sleep at night because of the traffic on the street.

   a. water pollution   b. noise pollution   c. land pollution

2. The city's parks are too dirty for families to have picnics.

   a. land pollution   b. air pollution   c. light pollution

3. Hundreds of birds are hurt when they fly into buildings.

   a. light pollution   b. air pollution   c. noise pollution

4. The smoke from the cars and buses hurts our eyes.

   a. water pollution   b. air pollution   c. land pollution

5. Most of the fish in the lake are dead.

   a. water pollution   b. noise pollution   c. air pollution

I. **List some subjects students can study to learn about protecting the environment. Discuss in small groups.**

School Curriculum: Environment

J. **What new information did you learn from watching the video? Compare your answers in small groups.**

STAND OUT VOCABULARY LIST

PRE-UNIT
Greetings 3
Numbers 7
Study verbs
listen 9
read 9
speak 9
write 9

UNIT 1
Personal information
age 14
divorced 16
height 17
marital status 14
married 16
single 16
weight 17
Hairstyle
curly 19
long 19
short 19
straight 19
wavy 19
Family
aunt 21
brother 20
children 21
daughter 21
father 21
granddaughter 21
grandfather 21
grandmother 21
grandson 21
husband 21
mother 21
nephew 21
niece 21
parents 20
sister 20
son 20
uncle 21
wife 21
Hobbies
books 23
computers 23
games 23
movies 23
music 23
parks 23
restaurants 23

sports 23
TV 23

UNIT 2
Stores
bookstore 39
clothing store 39
convenience store 39
department store 39
shoe store 39
supermarket 39
Money
bill 42
check 43
dime 42
nickel 42
penny 42
quarter 42
Clothing
baseball cap 44
belt 47
blouse 44
coat 44
dress 44
hat 44
pants 47
sandals 47
shorts 47
skirt 44
sneakers 44
socks 44
suit 44
sweater 44
tie 44
T-shirt 44
Colors
black 47
blue 47
brown 47
green 47
orange 47
red 47
white 47
yellow 47
Adjectives
big 51
plaid 50
large 50
medium 50
new 50
small 50

striped 50
used 50

UNIT 3
Food and meals
apples 66
avocados 65
bread 66
breakfast 62
carrots 65
cereal 63
cheeseburger 75
cookies 66
cucumbers 66
dinner 62
eggs 63
french fries 63
fried chicken 63
ground beef 65
hamburger 63
hot dog 76
lunch 62
milk 65
mustard 69
oranges 73
peanut butter 65
potato chips 66
roast beef 63
salad 74
sandwich 63
side order 74
soda 65
spaghetti 63
toast 63
tomatoes 65
yogurt 66
Containers/Measurements
bag 69
bottle 69
box 69
can 69
gallon 79
jar 69
package 69
pound 66

UNIT 4
Housing
apartment 86
backyard 91
balcony 91

bathroom 89
bedroom 89
carport 102
condominium 86
deck 91
dining room 90
driveway 91
electricity 93
family room 91
front porch 91
front yard 91
garage 91
gas 93
hall 91
kitchen 90
living room 90
mobile home 86
stairs 91
swimming pool 91
utilities 93
yard 91
Furniture
bathtub 98
bed 98
chair 98
coffee table 100
end table 100
lamp 100
painting 100
refrigerator 98
sofa 98
trash can 99

UNIT 5
Place in the community
bank 116
bus station 117
city hall 117
dentist's office 115
doctor's office 115
DMV (Department of
   Motor Vehicles) 116
high school 117
hospital 115
hostel 115
hotel 115
library 114
mall 120
motel 115
museum 119
park 115

playground 115
police station 114
post office 116
tennis courts 115
zoo 117
Directions
across from 121
around the corner 121
between 121
go straight 119
next to 121
on the corner 121
straight ahead 117
turn left 117
turn around 117
turn right 117

UNIT 6
Body parts
arm 139
back 139
chest 139

ear 139
eyes 139
foot (feet) 139
hand 139
head 138
leg 139
mouth 139
neck 139
nose 139
stomach 139
tooth (teeth) 139
Health
ambulance 147
backache 143
cold 142
cough 142
emergency 147
fever 138
flu 142
headache 141
lozenges 144
muscle ache 142

runny nose 141
pain reliever 144
sore throat 141
syrup 144
stomachache 143

UNIT 7
Jobs
busboy 170
cook/chef 163
mail carrier 168
mechanic 162
nurse 162
office worker 162
server 162
teller 162
Employment
application 177
benefits 165
cashier 163
custodian 163
experience 165

full-time 165
interview 171
part-time 165
secretary 163
teacher 163

UNIT 8
Education
adult school 192
Associate's Degree 192
Bachelor's Degree 192
college 192
degree 192
diploma 192
GED (General Education
Development) 192
goal 198
junior college 192
life skills 189
trade school 192
university 192

STAND OUT IRREGULAR VERB LIST

Base Verb	Simple Past	Base Verb	Simple Past
be	was, were	give	gave
bring	brought	go	went
build	built	have	had
buy	bought	make	made
choose	chose	meet	met
come	came	put	put
do	did	read	read
drive	drove	see	saw
drink	drank	send	sent
draw	drew	sleep	slept
eat	ate	speak	spoke
feel	felt	teach	taught
find	found	write	wrote

STAND OUT GRAMMAR REFERENCE

Simple Present: *Be*

Subject	*Be*	Information	Example sentence
I	am	43 years old	I **am** 43 years old.
He, She	is	single from Argentina	He **is** single. (Roberto **is** single.) She **is** from Argentina. (Gabriela **is** from Argentina.)
We, You, They	are	single married from Russia	We **are** single. You **are** married. They **are** from Russia.

Simple Present

Subject	Verb	Example sentence
I, You, We, They	eat like need want make	I **eat** tacos for lunch. You **like** eggs for breakfast. We **need** three cans of corn. They **want** three boxes of cookies. I **make** sandwiches for lunch.
He, She, It	eats likes needs wants makes	He **eats** pizza for dinner. She **likes** tomato soup. He **needs** three pounds of tomatoes. She **wants** two bottles of water. She **makes** sandwiches for Duong.

Simple Present

Subject	Verb	Example sentence
It My leg My arm My foot My head	hurts	My leg **hurts.** My arm **hurts.** My head **hurts.**
They My legs My arms My feet My ears	hurt	My legs **hurt.** My feet **hurt.** My ears **hurt.**

Simple Present

Subject	Verb	Example sentence
I, You, We, They	work	I **work** in an office.
He, She, It	works	He **works** in a restaurant.

Negative Simple Present

Subject	Negative	Verb	Example sentence
I, You, We, They	do not (don't)	work	I **don't work** in an office. You **don't work** in a restaurant.
He, She, It	does not (doesn't)		He **doesn't work** in a school. She **doesn't work** in a hospital.

Simple Present: *Have*

Subject	*Have*	Example sentence
I, You, We, They	have	I **have** a headache. You **have** a sore throat.
He, She, It	has	She **has** a stomachache. He **has** a fever.

Negative Simple Present: *Have*

Subject	Negative	*Have*	Example sentence
I, You, We, They	do not (don't)	have	I **don't have** a headache. You **don't have** a sore throat.
He, She, It	does not (doesn't)	have	She **doesn't have** a stomachache. He **doesn't have** a fever.

Simple Present

Subject	Adverb	*Verb*	Example sentence
I	always	write	I always **write** postcards.
He, She, It	often sometimes	eats	He rarely **eats** here.
You, We, They	rarely never	read	They never **read** the newspaper.

Simple Present: *Be*

Subject	*Be*		Example sentence
I	am		I **am** always early.
He, She, It	is	early late on time punctual	He **is** sometimes late. She **is** a good worker.
We, You, They	are		We **are** often early. You **are** never on time. They **are** always punctual.

Be Verb (Questions)

Question words	Be	Singular or plural noun	Example question
How much (money)	is	the dress the suit	How much **is** the dress? How much **is** the suit?
How much (money)	are	the socks the ties	How much **are** the socks? How much **are** the ties?

Be Verb (Answers)

Singular or plural noun or pronoun	Be	Example answer
It	is	It **is** $48. It**'s** $48. (The dress **is** $48.) It **is** $285. It**'s** $285. (The suit **is** $285.)
They	are	They **are** $12. They**'re** $12. (The socks **are** $12.) They **are** $22. They**'re** $22. (The ties **are** $22.)

Questions and Yes/No Answers

Question	Yes	No
Do you want a hamburger?	Yes, I do.	No, I don't.
Do they want sandwiches?	Yes, they do.	No, they don't.
Does he want a sandwich?	Yes, he does.	No, he doesn't.
Does she want a hot dog?	Yes, she does.	No, she doesn't.

Questions with Can

Can	Subject	Base verb	Example question
Can	I you	help ask talk answer call	**Can** I help you? **Can** I ask you a question? **Can** I talk to you? **Can** you answer a question? **Can** you call me?

Present Continuous

Subject	Be Verb	Base + ing	Example sentence
I	am	talk + ing	I **am talking** on the phone.
You, We, They	are	read + ing	We **are making** an appointment.
He, She, It	is	make + ing move + ing	She **is moving** into a new apartment.

Present Continuous

Subject	*Be*	Base + *ing*	Time	Example sentence
I	am (I'm)	writing	right now today	I'm **writing** a letter right now.
He, She, It	is (she's)	eating		She's **eating** a sandwich.
You, We, They	are (they're)	reading		They're **reading** a book today.

Should

Subject	*should*	Base verb	Example sentence
I, You, He, She, It, We, They	should	rest	You **should** rest.
		stay	He **should** stay home.
		go	They **should** see a doctor.
		take	I **should** take pain relievers.
			We **should** take cough syrup.

Should (Negative)

Subject	*should*	Base verb	Example sentence
I, You, He, She, It, We, They	should not (shouldn't)	drive	You **shouldn't** drive and take this medicine.
		drink	He **shouldn't** drink alcohol with this medicine.
		go	We **shouldn't** go out.

Simple Past: Regular Verbs

Subject	Base verb + *ed*		Example sentence
I, You, He, She, It, We, They	cleaned	tables	I **cleaned** tables.
	cooked	hamburgers	You **cooked** hamburgers.
	prepared	breakfast	He **prepared** breakfast.
	delivered	packages	She **delivered** packages.
	counted	the money	I **counted** the money.
	helped	other workers	We **helped** other workers.
	moved	to the United States	They **moved** to the United States.

Simple Past: *Be*

Subject	Be		Example sentence
I, He, She, It	was	a mail carrier	I **was** a mail carrier.
We, You, They	were	happy	You **were** happy.

Simple Past: *Be*

Subject	Be		Example sentence
I, He, She, It	was	early late	I **was** early yesterday. He **was** often late. She **was** always on time.
We, You, They	were	on time punctual	We **were** early on Saturday. You **were** on time today. They **were** never punctual.

Regular Past Tense Verbs

Base	Simple past
study	studied
participate	participated
help	helped
listen	listened
watch	watched
practice	practiced
learn	learned

Irregular Past Tense Verbs

Base	Simple past
come	came
see	saw
write	wrote
speak	spoke
read	read
teach	taught

Verb + Infinitive

Subject	Verb	Infinitive	Example sentence
I, You, We, They	like want need	to read to travel to work to talk to handle to study	I like **to read**. You want **to travel**. We need **to work** alone. They like **to talk** on the phone.
He, She, It	likes wants needs		He likes **to handle** money. She wants **to study**.

Verb + Noun

Subject	Verb	Noun	Example sentence
I, You, We, They	like want need	cars computer books school food	I like **cars**. You want a **computer**. We need **books**. They like **school**.
He, She, It	likes wants needs		He likes **computers**. She wants **food**.

Future with *Going to*

Subject	*Going to*	Base verb	Example sentence
I	am going to (I'm going to)	learn listen	I **am going to** learn English.
You, We, They	are going to (you're/we're/they're going to)	practice read speak	We **are going to** practice English.
He, She, It	is going to (he's/she's going to)	study write	She **is going to** speak English.

Future with *Will*

Subject	*Will*	Base	Example sentence
I, You, He, She, It We, They	will	study work get married	I **will** study every day. She **will** work hard. They **will** get married.

PHOTO CREDITS

STAND OUT SKILLS INDEX

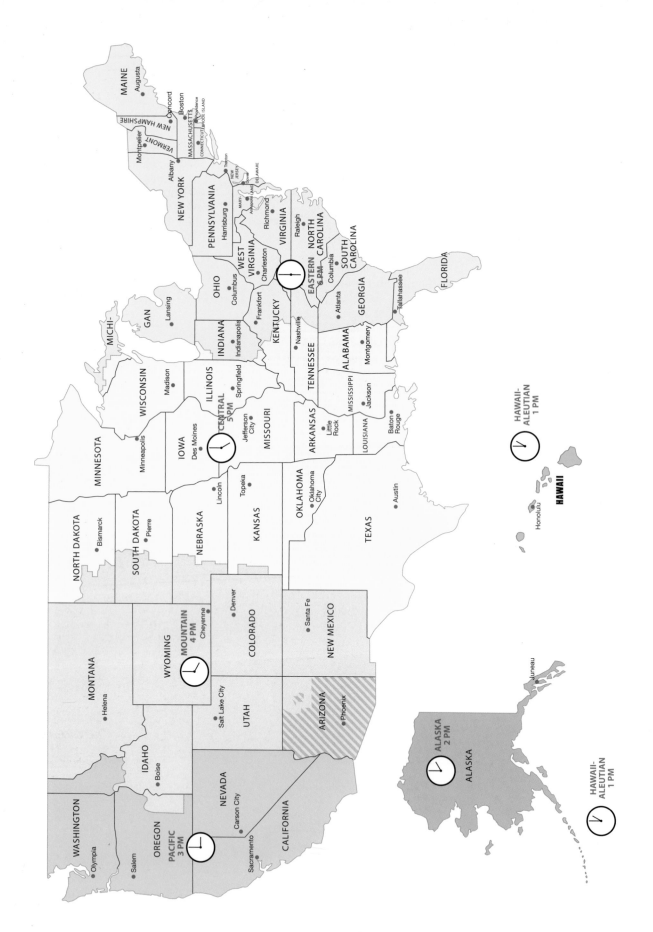